"this business has legs"

"this business has legs"

HOW I USED INFOMERCIAL
MARKETING TO CREATE
THE $100,000,000
***THIGHMASTER*®** CRAZE
EXERCISER

AN ENTREPRENEURIAL
ADVENTURE STORY

Peter Bieler

WITH
SUZANNE
COSTAS

New York • *Chichester* • *Brisbane* • *Toronto* • *Singapore*

To Randee

Who has inspired and shared all the best years of my life

Acknowledgments

Magnificent efforts by many people, in addition to the ones mentioned in this book, made the ThighMaster campaign a success.

Scott Wallin helped set up the company and steer it in the early days. My attorney Michael Wolf was instrumental in the negotiations that shaped the company. I was very dependent on another superb lawyer, Anthony LeWinter, during the difficult negotiations that attended my departure three years later. Gordon Stulberg, a generous man whose coattails have helped many young entrepreneurs to get a toe-hold, made the important introductions that birthed the company.

John Pike came on board after Randy Akers to manage our sales operation. Barry Entous, Marcia Sweet, and Dale Von Seggern were the accounting experts who helped keep the company on track during the difficult period of explosive growth. Karen Sykes ran a very efficient sales support staff. Ardie McDonald was superb in consumer relations. The list is long. I wish there was room to thank everyone involved. This is a very personal telling of an experience shared by many. I hope at least I have done credit to their memories of the time.

Ovation was also a virtual corporation, totally dependent on outsourcing to survive, much less flourish, when the ThighMaster campaign took off. We had a terrific team, including: Larry Bouchard and Tim Litle at Litle & Co., who did our credit-card processing; Rollie Froehlig at National Fulfillment; George Smith at West Telemarketing; Larry Schneiderman at Corinthian Media, helped by Arthur Yelsey, now at MediaSpot; Jess Joseph at NSI who ran our print ads; and Ben Giordano at Media Syndication Global.

Bob Todd offered crucial encouragement at the time I was trying to make the difficult decision to launch a retail operation.

Randee's and my good friend, the screenwriter Laurie Craig, first suggested that I write this book and kept encouraging me to do it, even when it was an unformed concept and an unlikely project.

When I finally took her up on the suggestion, I contacted my friend John Javna, who helped me get set in the new-to-me world of New York publishing. The well-named Faith Hamlin championed the book when it was just a vague idea. This is not the usual business book, and Janet Coleman, our editor at Wiley, was courageous to sign it up, and equally so to keep pushing and pushing for it all along the tortuous path to publication. Susan Bencuya checked our facts, saving us from embarrassment more than once.

My daughters Holly and Lacey are very young and not entirely happy about the time I have taken away from playing with them to work hard at getting this manuscript ready. Thanks, girls. Looking forward to getting your reaction when you read it in ten years.

The project would have died in its earliest stages if my wife Randee had not rescued the book proposal before it went out to publishers. She generously took time away from her own busy writing schedule to completely restructure it. This book would not be in your hands now without her intervention. During the writing, she filled in for my absence from the family, kept encouraging me, and offered valuable editing suggestions. I am lucky she is both my wife and partner.

During the writing, three friends also offered valuable editing input. Thank you Laurie Craig, Nancy Peter, and Jim McNamara. Suzanne's friend Susan Feldman also read it carefully and suggested many valuable line edits that we gratefully used.

This book was written in a bicoastal collaboration using phone and fax. I worked early mornings, and Suzanne worked late at night. We both worked weekends, and we both imposed unconscionably on our families. Suzanne's husband Barry Borak was Mr. Mom for their daughter Allegra for months on end. Thanks to both father and daughter for their patience, and to her nanny Nicola Irish.

The incidents and characters which make up this story are vivid in my memory, and I have described them frequently to friends. But there is a world of difference between telling a story and shaping it to be compelling for a reader, as anyone who has sat down to write a memoir knows. Point-of-view, pacing, scene setting, and construction are suddenly major concerns, demanding insightful choices, or your narrative is derailed. Without a talented cowriter, your story will not find an audience.

Suzanne Costas is a dream collaborator. She demanded clarity where I might have been satisfied with fuzzy mumbling. She ransacked my memory for telling details to bring scenes alive. She leaned on the delete key when I droned on. And in those inevitable dark hours when a deadline was looming, the collaborators tired, and the page empty, she laughed and got the job done.

Many people are responsible for the success of the ThighMaster campaign. I am responsible for the content of this book. But if you are beguiled by the telling of this story, thank Suzanne.

Contents

"this business has legs"

Introduction

John Lennon quipped that the Beatles were more famous than Jesus. I won't make *that* mistake.

I will say, however, that if you haven't heard of the ThighMaster exerciser, you've been shipwrecked on a deserted island or you're still in Pampers; either way, you won't be reading this book. It's safe to assume, therefore, that you're acquainted with the product, that you probably recall the ad campaign featuring Suzanne Somers, that you may even have a ThighMaster under your bed or have given one as a gift to someone you love or as a joke to someone you don't.

Me? I'm the guy behind the ThighMaster success, a dubious distinction unless you appreciate the difficulties inherent in capturing the attention of the whole country, in selling 6 million

ThighMasters in less than two years and doing it all without a war chest the size of General Motors.

In fact, the phenomenon that grossed over $100 million started in a modest office with three people.

I discovered the ThighMaster when it was leading an unglamorous life as an upperbody exerciser at a fitness ranch. The first thing I did was give it sex appeal. I defined it as a shaping and toning thigh exerciser for women. Then I promoted it like crazy. I launched a national media campaign using infomercial advertising. But I had more in mind than creating the next Chia Pet promotion. My goal was retail.

Why? Because only one person in five who sees your ad with an 800 number and wants your product will actually phone in an order. The other four will wait until they can purchase it in a store—they just have to hold something before they buy it. These are the folks you want, the dyed-in-the wool retail shoppers. The phone-in buyers pay for the media. The ad runs frequently. Those retail shoppers start asking for the product where they shop. And all of a sudden, Kmart, Wal-Mart, all the big retail operations that it takes most manufacturers years to get into, are courting you. You've hit the jackpot.

The ThighMaster campaign was the first major hit designed around this strategy. What did it mean? Now small companies had a way to buy national advertising to establish mass-market brand awareness.

Just what I was looking for.

In a family of artists and academics, I always wanted to be a businessman. When I bought a Pepsi after school, I was aware that there was a person behind that product, someone whose company had managed to capture the public's attention so that all over the country, all over the *world,* people bought the product almost instinctively. What an achievement, I thought. Is it any wonder that two of my favorite books are David Ogilvy's *Confessions of an Advertising Man* and Jerry Della Femina's *From Those Won-*

derful Folks Who Gave You Pearl Harbor? They sit on my desk, and they're dog-eared.

My fascination with how advertising campaigns create brand names that everybody knows and trusts led me to a job at Procter & Gamble. I didn't expect to stay long; I saw myself as an entrepreneur starting a mainstream consumer products company. At P&G, I learned the mechanics of brand creation. I also learned that launching a national brand required a big, compelling advertising campaign, expensive beyond belief but absolutely necessary. I put my small-business fantasy on hold. I moved to Hollywood. What can I say? I liked films.

I worked for years in the entertainment industry and had some success and a lot of good adventures. Then, when I was 45 years old, I stumbled upon the newly born infomercial industry.

It was a carnival business, for sure, but it had some redeeming qualities—chief among them, terrific cash flow. Here was a way to finance a media campaign without millions of dollars in the bank. And it didn't take much money to get going. I swallowed hard and jumped in.

There's no doubt about it, infomercials are an odd way of selling. Thirty minutes devoted to a hair accessory or a new-fangled mop seems a bit much (though not for products like Windows 95 and Phillips CD Interactive). And the industry has been roundly criticized for peddling schlock. I've no tolerance for shoddy products or for deceptive advertising and false claims. Here I am in perfect agreement with P.T. Barnum, erroneously associated with the slogan, "There's a sucker born every minute." Barnum was one of the first American business people to appreciate publicity, but he drew the line at cheating the public: Once the customers are lined up, never fail to give 'em their money's worth. People often ask me if the ThighMaster works, and I always say the same thing: It does if you use it.

There are those who say infomercials work because people are vain and stupid and gullible. I disagree. Infomercials work because people are isolated. Isolation is a fact of modern life and explains why all kinds of people, yes, even people with college degrees, buy off television. Infomercials work because we're social creatures; we like to feel that we're part of something, even if it's a television audience. Marshall McLuhan was correct when he observed that television was "above all, a medium that demands a creatively participant response." I'd say that goes double for infomercials. Not only do the ads demand a reaction, they push you toward the telephone.

You'll hear many arguments against going into this business: Only one in seven shows succeed; media costs are rising; celebrity royalties are rising; margins are thinning; and, unlike the early days of infomercials, competition is cutthroat. My response is that it's got a better chance of success than many businesses you could start, and, if you succeed, the payoff is a lot higher than most.

I'm not embarrassed to have made a fortune with the Thigh-Master. (I loved the jokes on *Letterman* and *Leno*. The more jokes, the more ThighMasters we sold.) We made a good product and people bought it.

Was I surprised? Not at all. Some products capture the public's fancy by accident. I know the guy who promoted the Pet Rock, and he was as surprised as anybody by the product's success. But the ThighMaster craze was no accident. It was deliberate. It was calculated. And it can be repeated.

That's an important message in this book. Any manufacturer, importer, or inventor with a product that has mass appeal can launch a national TV ad campaign, largely or wholly paid for by the people who phone in and buy off the 800 number. Forget the *what* of infomercials—the Ginzu knives, the smokeless ashtrays. Focus on the *how,* the process that can put a national TV campaign within the reach of even tiny companies. A campaign that can catapult a product into the big leagues as a brand-name star.

Who should be using these techniques? Anyone with a mass-market product that has a distinct advantage over the competition that would be compelling in a TV ad. CD software manufacturers, for instance. Book publishers. Clothing designers. Manufacturers of household appliances, furnishings, sporting goods, and health and beauty products.

But wait! There's more! as they say on TV.

6

The infomercial industry also offers excellent opportunities for start-ups. The initial investment is relatively low. The industry has dependable vendors to handle every aspect of the campaign and help newcomers steer clear of big mistakes. It's a cash business. You get your money before you ship your product. And best of all, when you have a success, the cash flow is quick and massive. This book shows you how to get there.

There's something else about infomercials that attracts a whole different crowd—*they're long*. That's why Chrysler, Apple, Mattel, and other Fortune 1000 companies are using 30-minute ads to explain the features and benefits and innovations of their new products. A 30-second spot gives you a flattering snapshot of a product. A 30-minute infomercial is a full-blown press conference. Marketing executives take note.

But this book is not just about marketing strategies. It takes you behind the scenes of a wildly successful media campaign that began with no money, no product, no experience. I share all my secrets.

It did not come easy. Writing a business plan and finding financing were tough enough. The unexpected challenge was overcoming doubt and discouragement. So many times I had to jump-start myself out of inertia. I had to stare down a sense of futility. I needed to recover from heartbreak and betrayal I never expected.

I have laid out strategies for success in this book, including all the how-to information someone new to the infomercial business will need to prosper. But I've also told a very personal story. The inner struggles of a start-up entrepreneur are as formidable as the outer ones.

I promise you a tale of marketing, mania, and the American Dream; a story replete with curveballs, contradictions, and surprises, set against the backdrop of a markedly unusual (read bizarre) industry.

Stay tuned.

CHAPTER · 1

A Hollywood Adventure

We live in the Hollywood Hills, in the once illustrious neighborhood that boasted Gloria Swanson, Hedy Lamarr, and Cecil B. deMille. The movie stars and moguls who settled here during that golden age built grand mansions overlooking acres of lemon groves. After the stock market crashed, more than a few estates—mostly those owned by industrialists—were sold and subdivided, and up popped the more modest homes that cover the hillsides now.

Our house is one of them. It's not high enough to have a view of the city, but from our daughter's bedroom window you can see the famous Hollywood sign. (She thinks we had it built for her. Her name is Holly.) When out-of-towners visit us, we take them to Holly's room to see the sign. It's like a tour. Everyone says the same thing, that it looks small, which it does from this distance. Yet, somehow, they're satisfied.

Hollywood is like that.

Lots of stars still live here. A few of our neighbors—we don't actually *know* them, I'm just dropping names—include Nicolas Cage, whose gray Ferrari vrooms past our house on its way up the hill; Lily Tomlin, who owns W.C. Fields' house; and newcomer Brad Pitt, who bought Elvira's manse. (Yes, the buxom horror movie hostess.) Sinead O'Connor almost bought the house next door to us, its principal attraction being the geodesic dome in the backyard. My wife Randee is glad she didn't.

Randee's a writer. She was worried about practice sessions.

We were living here when I got the job at Landsburg to produce instructional and special interest videos. Alan Landsburg's the guy who brought the hype of carney sideshows to prime time with *In Search Of* with Leonard Nimoy and *That's Incredible,* then riveted the nation with tearjerkers like *Adam,* the story about a murdered child that awoke the nation to the problem of missing children, and *Bill,* where Mickey Rooney plays a retarded man. When Alan hired me, I was producing comedy tapes for another company. (Most nights I hung out at The Comedy Store on Sunset Boulevard. I caught David Letterman, once, when he was still an unknown. I asked him to do a video, but he declined. Politely.)

I got into the business in the early '80s when I noticed that the video store at Hollywood and Orange, across the street from Grauman's Chinese Theater, had a paltry number of videos for sale. I did some research and confirmed a hunch. It wasn't just this store that needed product; they all did.

While still under contract to produce comedy tapes, I decided to form a limited partnership to produce informational videos. So I approached Alan. Part of the story I spun was that video stores would become the libraries of the future. It wasn't just hype; I truly believed it. I thought people would be eager to learn a new language, improve their golf game, catch up on the latest health trend, or tour Europe from the comfort of their La-Z-Boys. I urged Alan to take advantage of his position. He had studios, lights, cameras—*everything.* All he needed was a producer. To my surprise, he put up *all* the money and brought the business—and me—in-house.

Like a lot of people, I was wrong about the future of video. The bubble burst before my eyes when I was at a post-production house editing a video for Landsburg. I saw a guy stacking film reels in the hallway. "What's going on?" I asked casually. He told me they were old movies to be transferred to video. That's why the place seemed so busy. The studios had opened their film vaults. It was only a matter of time before Myrna Loy and William Powell knocked *The Eight-Week Cholesterol Cure* off the shelf.

I should've quit Landsburg that instant and opened a video store. Or become a distributor. But I persevered.

As a consequence, I missed a rare opportunity. The future of video was in renting *Tootsie* for three bucks, not shelling out $19.95 for a tape about avoiding heart disease. Given the choice between information and entertainment, people chose entertainment.

I was right to stay with TV, though. Just as Marshall McLuhan predicted, TV has become the electronic campfire. We gather around it to listen to our storytellers, hear the news, and share gossip about celebrities and the eccentrics in our midst. Is it the least bit remarkable that TV is increasingly where we shop? According to a Leisure Trends/Gallup survey conducted for the National Infomercial Marketing Association (NIMA), 77 percent of all Americans have now viewed an infomercial, whether long-form (30 minutes) or short-form (one or two minutes), and 23 percent have made an infomercial purchase, up almost ¼ from 1994.

The dollars add up. The Direct Marketing Association commissioned a study from The WEFA Group (Wharton Economic Forecasting Associates) on the size of the direct-response industry, which found short- and long-form infomercials, and shopping channels generated $9.6 billion in sales in 1995. Infomercials represented more than $6.5 billion of that figure. By comparison, the total box office take for all feature films released in both the United States and Canada in 1995 was $5.4 billion, a figure that implies that infomercials are one of the most profitable forms of American entertainment.

And TV direct response is projected to grow 9.7 percent annually between now and the year 2000, as opposed to only 5.5 percent for sales overall. The point is, Americans watch a lot of TV, and, more and more, they're watching infomercials.

For me, the path that led to success was long and meandering, but I learned lessons that were crucial and honed the leadership skills that just weren't there when I was in my twenties. Let me digress for a moment and tell you about this odyssey.

My father despised television. The first and last TV we owned was gone within two weeks, right after I mentioned to him I wanted to watch wrestling. Born in Lausanne, Switzerland, he was a post-impressionist painter of great acclaim in Canada. We lived in a university town, halfway between Montreal and Toronto. He taught at the college and came from a family of professors. My mother, a Quebecoise, designed furniture and spoke with a French accent until the day she died.

It was an unlikely background for an infomercial producer.

Not a bad thing.

For some professions, the way is straight. My best friend, as a kid, always wanted to be a doctor. He graduated from medical school at 25, was practicing by 30, and lived happily ever after. Done deal. But there are some vocations where it pays to have lived a bit before you get going. One is novelist. Another is entrepreneur.

Right out of college, I devoted my life to spiritual contemplation and ascetic self-denial. Not quite a monk, but close. I went to Scotland and took an M.A. in philosophy at the University of Glasgow. Philosophy was the closest I could get to Eastern religions at a traditional university in the 1960s. (This was before the Beatles discovered the sitar.) I was a great fan of Somerset Maugham's *The Razor's Edge,* about a young man trying to find himself by refusing to live according to society's expectations.

Like Maugham's Larry Darrell, I wanted to go to India. Twenty-two and I sought inner peace, not excitement. Go figure.

Anyway, the Hindus believe that the world we see around us is no more real than a dream. What matters is the voyage of your soul. That appealed to me. It was also a do-it-yourself religion. No clergy, no mass. You meditated; you gave up meat, alcohol, and sex. You practiced silence. It required enormous discipline. But I liked the challenge. I also liked being in charge of my fate.

I moved to Paris because that's what Larry Darrell did. I lived in a garret, with a sliver view of the Eiffel Tower. I took a job as a bank teller, breaking my vow of silence between 9 A.M. and 5 P.M. In my free time, I meditated or read.

I was really into it.

I saved my money to buy an overland ticket to India. But when I'd saved enough, I put it off. I found excuses not to go to the travel agent. Finally, I faced the truth. I wasn't cut out to be a monk. After years of meditation, I was stalled. I had been listening to my spiritual side for a long time. Now I decided to listen to my other side. What I heard was a big surprise—marketing. It made sense in a way, given my fascination with ad campaigns going back to my childhood.

In the 1960s, marketing had an intellectual aura. It was a new science. You had sixty seconds to leave an indelible impression, a task which demanded creative problem-solving. I was good at puzzles, and I'd always been more intrigued by the TV ads than the programs. The ads seemed more inventive. What the heck, it looked more fun than banking or teaching Eastern religions.

Meditation to marketing. No road map existed for a career switch like that. But contemplating my options in solitude, I kept coming back to marketing. It was a strong feeling, and it emerged whenever I took the time to let my mind lie still. Many of my most important decisions came that way then.

I applied for a job as an assistant brand manager for Procter & Gamble at its Canadian headquarters in Toronto. P & G was a hot company. It had just introduced the first disposable diaper, Pampers. On the strength of an endorsement from the American Dental Association, its Crest toothpaste pulled ahead of Colgate. It entered the coffee business with its 1963 purchase of J. A. Folger

& Co. That same year it brought out Head and Shoulders shampoo. Added to the perennial strength of Tide and their big traditional soap business, it looked like a company on the move. By
1965, sales of P & G's products had reached over $2 billion.
Impressive.

To my delight, they offered me a job.

I worked on some big campaigns. With great interest I watched
P & G spend millions over 18 months to roll out Scope in Canada.
Up till then, no one worried too much about fresh breath. Sure,
there were Listerine and Lavoris, but they dominated a small
market with minimal advertising. Then P & G came along and created anxiety about halitosis. From Vancouver to Halifax, people
reached for Scope. P & G had *created* a need, *created* a market.
Amazing.

The most talked-about campaign at P & G was the one that
helped make Duncan Hines the best-selling cake mix in North
America. Until the 1960s, the ready-made cake mix market had
been dominated by General Mills' Betty Crocker. There were a
lot of things you could say about a cake mix. It was quick. It was
easy. It was fail-safe. You could bake cakes you never dared bake
before. All of those claims were true, but all had been used by
Betty Crocker. Ah, but here was something interesting. Although cake mixes had improved over the years, P & G's market
research revealed that many people still perceived them as dry
and tasteless. Why not respond to *that* concern? If the consumer
wanted a cake mix that was "moist as homemade," then Duncan
Hines needed to show that its product could meet that need. But
how?

The Duncan Hines brand managers gathered 50 housewives
into a room—P & G loved focus groups—to ask them about the
packaged cake mixes they used. After a few hours, one of the
ladies noted that if she could pick up the little extra crumbs off
the plate—if they stuck to her fork—then the cake was moist.
That's how the fork demo appeared on TV.

The commercial focused on one crucial claim. Duncan Hines
pulled ahead of the competition.

This lesson served me well years later when I created the Thigh-Master campaign: Good advertising shines a light on the most compelling facet of a product ("moist"). Bad advertising, in contrast, makes a claim that isn't true and then hopes the public won't notice. Banks often boast that their tellers are the friendliest and their lines are the shortest. It's a lie. Insurance companies claim to be compassionate. It's a crock. Almost as bad, an honest claim is made, but it's the wrong claim to make; it's not compelling to the buyers you're trying to reach. Gablinger's was the first company to invent lite beer. Alas, they advertised fewer calories. Beer-drinkers (read men) don't give a damn about their waistlines. Just pour another pitcher, Joe. Miller Lite got it right: "Tastes great; less filling!" Beer-drinkers across America rejoiced. Now they could drink even *more* beer!

But the most effective selling is invisible. The copy doesn't read like copy. Take the Maytag repairman. Randee and I bought a Maytag dishwasher a few years ago, and two months later it broke down. Staring at the idle machine, we blurted the same thing: "But it's a *Maytag!*" It just didn't seem possible. We had bought into the copy so totally that we had forgotten it *was* copy. This is not to say that Maytag doesn't make a good product. But the tale about the lonely repairman is just an exquisite way of stating what everyone wants in a washing machine—dependability. No doubt some copywriter hatched the fable one night in his Upper East Side apartment, probably over Chinese take-out. Next morning, he tore into the office, brandishing the copy. "I've got it. The repairman *hates* Maytag!"

So the challenge of marketing is to identify what's most compelling about your product and to *own* that claim. When you think of Volvo, you think safety. When you think of Federal Express, you think no screw-ups. When you think of ThighMaster, you think shapely hips and thighs.

Notice how all of the above are benefits, not features. A swiss army knife folds up neatly in your pocket—a nice *feature,* but a *benefit* is that it could save your life if you get lost in the woods. The ThighMaster exerciser can fit into your suitcase—again, a

17

nice feature, but the benefits are shapely hips and thighs. And before you ask what the most compelling benefit is, you must identify your target market (in the case of a pocket knife, it's campers; hobbyists; boys between 12 and 18). There's no use getting hung up on catchy lines and slogans before you know who you're talking to and what they want to hear.

All of the above were important to me in marketing Thigh-Master, and I learned it all at the University of Procter & Gamble. (Other graduates who've made their marks as entrepreneurs include Scott Cook, CEO of Intuit, and Steve Case, founder and CEO of America Online. P & G's training helps to sell anything.) As fledgling execs we were taught to approach marketing analytically, to take this mysterious process and break it down into discrete parts. There were specific steps to be followed. There was a procedure. That's how the company turned young men and women with liberal arts degrees, people like me, into marketing executives.

What Stanislavsky did for acting when he invented The Method, Procter & Gamble did for marketing.

It was an academic environment. Trainees were required to write their copy strategy on a single piece of paper, not an easy task. (Those secretaries who were good at squeezing margins were prized.) Memos were brutally critiqued.

Even routine decisions were subjected to a great deal of deliberation.

I remember a room the size of a closet with shelves and shelves of premiums—chef aprons, salad bowls, measuring cups, salad spoons, rain hats. If you were writing a mail-in offer—you know, two box tops and $2 gets you a set of salad bowls—you had to back up your copy strategy with research. So the guy in the room handed you the premium *and* a 200-page document, a computer printout of responses from focus groups. You pored over this material for days, trying to determine whether the demographics of, say, lower Quebec supported salad bowls or rain hats. And, if you ended up with rain hats, you still had to decide on pink or blue!

After a couple of years, it started to drive me crazy.

. . .

The movies kept me sane. Going to them, thinking about them, reading books about filmmaking. This was the era of Young-Turk directors such as Richard Lester, who did the Beatles films, and the new-wave films of François Truffaut. Dennis Hopper's *Easy Rider* stunned everyone, but what got Hollywood's attention were its boffo box-office receipts. The old guys almost choked on their cigars. Doris Day and Rock Hudson movies were history.

The Graduate, directed by the then-young Mike Nichols, made a huge impression on me. The movie spoke to my generation as none had before. Even the music was *our* music. After seeing it, I bought an 8mm camera and shot a movie at night, after work. I'm certain I was the only Procter & Gamble employee writing, producing, and directing a movie in his spare time. It was a lugubrious little tale about lost love, pathetically titled *When Will the Morning Come?* The lead actress became my girlfriend. The process of designing one more tear-off campaign for Crest paled in comparison.

Then I applied to film school. Apparently I showed some promise. I was accepted at USC, one of the hardest programs to get into—even Spielberg was rejected. (That they took me and not him does make you wonder.) After I graduated, I had a hard time breaking into the industry, so I took a job managing a rock and roll concert hall in downtown Los Angeles. (Bear in mind that most film school graduates don't end up making movies. How many drama school graduates get jobs on Broadway?) My break came when Quinn Martin, king of the white-bread '70s cop shows, rented my concert hall for three days to shoot some scenes for the series *Manhunter.* During the shoot, their location manager quit.

I put a call through to QM's head of production, and he took the call right away. (Sure, he did; I was a landlord in a position to stop his shoot. He'd never returned any of my calls when I was just another film-school grad looking for a job.)

Was there a problem? he asked anxiously. No, I replied, except that his location manager just quit. I offered my services and he told me to come in.

The next day was the interview I had been preparing for the entire year since leaving film school. I had *a lot* of reasons why he should hire me. And I made him sit there and listen to every single one of them. When I finished, I waited for a reaction. None came. He sat behind his desk with his chin in his hand, not a muscle moving, his eyes half-closed. It was about seven o'clock in the evening. He had dozed off. He finally looked up and mumbled something about getting back to me. I left in a total funk. I'd blown it.

I dragged myself to his office the following day without an appointment. He made me wait eight hours in his reception room before he finally admitted me. This time, I kept my pitch short and punchy, therefore compelling. "Mr. Alston," I said, "You need a location manager *right now*. I need a job *right now*. I'm trained and qualified. Please hire me."

The next day I reported to CBS Studio Center. I was in.

It's easier to say too much than just enough. I never forgot the lesson about keeping your marketing pitch *simple*.

I also worked at Columbia Pictures. What a hoot. Remember the movie *The Deep?* I was the location manager. Spent months in Bermuda with Jackie Bisset. I also worked on the Oscar-winning *Bound for Glory* and, at MGM, on *The Champ,* starring Jon Voight and Ricky Schroeder.

During the filming of *The Champ,* I realized that the longer I worked as a location/production manager, the harder it would be to get a job "above the line." In Hollywood, technicians and support staff work "below the line," and, generally speaking, the only way they move up is to move out. So I quit my job to become associate director of the American Film Institute.

It was a strategic move; the Institute is the darling of the film business. It hands out prestigious film awards and runs the most respected film school in the country. (Randee's a grad.) I attended cocktail parties and premieres. I forged relationships.

After a few years I left and, like every other independent producer in Hollywood, put together some film packages and tried to peddle them. One of the great, mystifying things about raising capital is the number of people willing to talk to you who don't have a nickel to spare, or, just as bad, who have no intention of investing in anything, anytime, anywhere. I can't tell you how many hours I spent in well-appointed living rooms in Brentwood and Beverly Hills, only to learn I'd been wasting my time. I guess it's flattering to be courted. It's an ego boost.

Anyway, I gave up trying to raise money to make a movie when, as I mentioned before, I wandered into the video store at Hollywood Boulevard and Orange. The store's empty shelves spelled opportunity to me. I would produce special-interest videos. I saw myself as a teacher, bringing instruction to the masses. I don't know. But I got excited.

So, as you know, Alan Landsburg hired me as a video producer. This was 1986, the same year Randee and I were married. It seemed a swell job. *Marketing and showbiz combined!* There was just one problem. It wasn't showbiz and it wasn't marketing. Okay, two problems.

My office was at the front of the building, where people sat at their desks all day—brows furrowed, fingers drumming, dreaming up new ideas to pitch to the networks. It was like a think tank and, except for the hum of the air conditioning, quiet as a library. Glamour? Forget about it. The building was a barn, decorated with remnants. Art? Posters of Gary Owens and Leonard Nimoy; of John Davidson, Kathy Lee Crosby and Fran Tarkenton, the three of them grinning like jack-o'-lanterns. Plants? A solitary rubber tree in the hallway. I stayed in my office as much as possible. I left the fluorescent lights off.

No one was buying my videos. The most popular (and I'm speaking in relative terms) was *The Eight-Week Cholesterol Cure,* based upon the best-selling book. The video featured talk show host Larry King. Because he'd had a heart attack, he could speak convincingly about the need to watch your diet and to exercise. Larry King or not, the video was causing no ripples in the marketplace because I had no budget for promotion or marketing. All this hard work, and the videos just sat on the shelf and collected dust. It was frustrating.

But someone was making money. *A lot* of money.

The *back* of the Landsburg building was bustling. There was a small sound stage that was jammed with lights, cameras, and a crush of people. In the room next door, people were busily typing and answering phones. In the evening, on my way out, an independent television crew would be coming in. It was very intense. I thought it was a telethon.

After a week of this, I stopped someone in the hallway. "What's going on?" I asked.

"Oh, we're filming an info-commercial," the man said, and hurried on. His name was Jim McNamara; he was one of the show's producers, and the man I'd eventually hire to write the copy for the ThighMaster ad. The next day, over a sandwich, he gave me the details.

A guy by the name of Tony Hoffman was renting the stage for $500 a day to produce a live, daily show called *Everybody's Money Matters*. It revolved around personal finance, but mainly it was about how to make money in real estate. This was the '80s, after all, and real estate was on fire. Hoffman was broadcasting live, five nights a week, 10 P.M. to 12 P.M. (1 A.M. to 3 A.M. EST). But the show had no commercials. *It* was a commercial. An infomercial. A *two-hour* ad.

I stayed late one night to watch the broadcast. It looked like a traditional talk show. A host sat behind a desk. A cohost sat in a chair next to him. There were chairs for guests. There were potted plants. There was a backdrop of Hollywood, including the Hollywood sign. The production was cheesy, though. It reeked of college television. But, being live, anything could happen. The atmosphere was charged.

The cohost, Bob Braun, played Ed McMahon to Hoffman's Carson. Braun was a television personality from Cincinnati, a former talk-show host who God had blessed with a deep voice, a chiseled jaw, and perfect hair. He was smooth; he reminded me of the Muppet character Guy Smiley. Bob knew his way around a TelePromp Ter; Tony, obviously, did not. Short, dark, chubby, with a Brooklyn accent, Tony had a background in sales, specifically mutual funds and life insurance. The contrast was striking: hale and hearty Midwesterner, abrasive New York Jew. But it worked: Women thought Braun was charming, and men figured Hoffman knew a bargain when he saw one. (Tom Vu's shows worked for similarly base reasons. Unemployed factory workers, seeing Vu and his bevy of bikini-clad babes lounging on the yacht, sneered, "Hell, if this *foreigner* can make a bundle in real estate, then so can I," and reached for the phone.)

The guests on *Everybody's Money Matters* were mostly get-rich-quick guys who'd written books about how to buy distressed properties, how to get low-interest government loans, and so forth. Now they offered cassette tapes on the same topics. (Tony got half their sales—but he sold his *own* tapes, too, from $70 to $400.) There were live phone calls from people with questions. ("Hi! This is Madge, from Cleveland. How do I buy a property out of probate?")

Tony spiced things up with celebrity guests, people like Phyllis Diller, Florence Henderson, and Hugh O'Brien.

The show attracted mostly a blue-collar audience. (Hoffman tells an amusing story. He was having dinner one night with Efram Zimbalist, Jr., a guest on the show, and Hoffman remarked, "Efram, everyone sitting in this restaurant knows who *you* are, while everyone waiting on us knows who *I* am.") By disguising sales as entertainment, Hoffman effectively converted viewers into buyers. The stars caught your attention, and the talk about money held it. Then came the "call to action," the urgent plea to "pick up the phone and dial our toll-free number. Operators are standing by." You dialed an 800 number to order the books and tapes. Which meant you talked to somebody in Omaha, Nebraska, where most of the big telemarketing companies are located.

It aired on Lifetime and reached only about 110,000 people a night. But Tony was on to something: *Success was measured not by the number of viewers, like normal television, but by sales.* And the cash register was ringing. On a good night, Tony would take in $80,000! And, remember, the media time was peanuts—$7,500 a broadcast. Fast, easy money. No wonder the infomercial business exploded.

23

Yet something else made me sit up and take notice, something too many people have overlooked about infomercials: Tony had a national ad campaign and didn't know it. Sure, it looked different than a Coke ad. But the end result was the same: brand awareness. He was exposing his product to the mass market through the most effective selling tool we've got: television. Tony was hawking real estate books but the strategy could apply to many different products. And it didn't take a genius to see that you could buy time on the other cable networks, not to mention maybe 50 broadcast stations, to reach millions of people instead of thousands.

The conventional wisdom at this time was that a company needed at least $200 million in sales to be able to afford a meaningful national TV campaign. Who was saying this? Marketing guru John Sculley for one, in his 1987 book called *Odyssey*, about running Pepsi and Apple.

But Tony's campaign didn't require deep pockets; it was self-sustaining.

Sculley was wrong.

Direct response was changing the rules of advertising. And retailing.

Sculley spoke from tradition. You hired Madison Avenue to dream up an ad, which cost a lot of dough. Then you waited, hoping people would run to the stores when they saw your commercial. If they did, the money landed in the store's cash registers. Eventually it wound its way back to you.

But direct response offered some short cuts. You didn't need Madison Avenue. Or the stores. You ran the infomercial on Monday, people ordered the product *on Monday,* and you saw your profits on Tuesday. It was a cash business. Your customers paid with credit cards and checks, so just a few days after a broadcast, you had all your sales receipts in hand. You could then turn right around and buy more air time and inventory.

The beauty of direct-response advertising was that it was self-financing; it was accessible to anyone.

To me.

About the time Tony showed up at the back of the Landsburg building, my video division was losing money. To become profitable, I needed to support the videos with marketing, but mine was a tiny operation without the budget to mount a meaningful campaign.

Then I started to put it together. Tony had a national TV campaign that cost little but all he cared about was whether his phones rang. I cared about the people who *didn't* call, all those people who saw a product in an infomercial and wanted it but would rather buy it in a store: the retail shoppers.

I hadn't done any marketing since my days at Procter & Gamble, but I knew I had a packaged consumer good and that the old P&G marketing rules would apply. There are two ways to get a new product into stores and onto the shelf: One is to have a massive sales force, badgering store managers for orders and bigger displays in high-traffic areas; the other is to create an advertising campaign that motivates people to ask for the product where they shop.

It was highly unlikely I was going to build a sales force; I worked for a television studio. That left advertising, the kind of advertising that costs a fortune. Luckily, I'd just discovered how to build a national campaign that was self-supporting. All I needed were cameras and lights, and that, Landsburg had in abundance.

I grew excited. I told Randee I wanted to propose an idea to Alan, actually, to Howard Lipstone, the company's president. Something unconventional. I explained to her that I wanted to make an infomercial for one of the videos we planned to produce.

"Like those ads on cable at I A.M.?" she asked. Randee's a night owl.

"Exactly. I haven't got enough of a marketing budget, right? You know, to really sell the videos. But with an infomercial, you don't need a marketing budget. You finance your campaign out of cash flow."

Randee knew a thing or two about selling. Before she went to film school, she'd been a copywriter for seven years for an ad agency in North Carolina. Selling was something she'd been good at. Farmers would hand over thousands of dollars for hydraulic hose because of what she wrote about it. Southern ladies would line up for lunch at restaurants her ads promoted.

Randee smiled. She got it.

And, boy, did I have the perfect product for an infomercial. I had just acquired the rights to do an exercise video using the Weider name. This is the Joe Weider who introduced Arnold Schwarzenegger to America, who runs the Mr. Olympia competition and publishes *Muscle & Fitness, Shape,* and *Flex.* Weider also makes gym and exercise equipment. Early on, they'd figured out it was more profitable to sell body-building magazines chockablock with ads for their own products than to distribute a catalogue for free. They were right. It was more profitable.

"The sculpted look is in," I told Randee. "I'll make an attractive infomercial, get an 800 number, and see if the phones ring."

She flashed me her go-get-'em grin, and I knew she meant it, but she was also worried. She recognized the signs. I was falling in love with a new business. Great timing. Randee was five months pregnant. Before the pregnancy, she'd been a successful screenwriter. She had herself a hot TV agent, and she was even nominated for an Oscar for a short film she wrote. But the pregnancy made her feel vulnerable. We were going to be a one-income family for a while, and she wasn't keen on my making a career change just then.

"What if Landsburg hates the idea of infomercials?" she asked.

"I'll find the money somewhere else."

I hoped I wouldn't have to, of course. Life would be simpler if Landsburg stepped up to the plate.

Alan and Howard are opposites. Alan is the creative one; bouncy and kinetic. He's a superb salesman. *Superb.* Howard moves slowly; he's methodical. His job is to watch the bottom line, to crunch the numbers. Pitching Howard on infomercials would be tough. They weren't in the ad business, and one of Howard's great strengths is knowing what business he is in and sticking to it.

And there was the office to deal with.

They shared one of those huge, open work spaces. Alan sat behind a monstrous, custom-built desk, big enough for three CEOs. Howard sat at a much smaller desk, right across from him. There was a ring of secretaries. There was the very real possibility of public humiliation.

I sat in one of the chairs facing Howard's desk and waited for him to get off the phone.

"Howard," I began. "I think one of the reasons you got involved in how-to videos was because of this facility. You've got cameras, lights, a studio. You've got everything required. And that's why we should be doing much more to sell them. What do you say we really go for it. Produce an infomercial for the Weider exercise video. You know, create a marketing campaign, buy the air time. Really *sell* it."

Howard has a low chair, so I always felt like I was talking to his computer. I couldn't really see him. I could hear him, though, tapping on his keypad.

"I really think the Weider name will create demand," I continued. I also told him about Tony Hoffman's show. About the cash flow in direct response.

Howard punched a couple more keys. Click, click, click. I peeked around the computer. His eyes shifted back and forth between me and his monitor, his bald spot shining under the fluorescent lights.

"That's not our business, Peter. TV is our business." He gave me his forced smile, which meant he was either bored or displeased.

I tried another tack.

"O.K. How about a dry test to reduce our risk?"

He looked up.

"We produce the ad for the video before we produce the video itself. We run the ad on TV, and if the phones light up, we know we've got something. We produce the video. If they don't light up, we stop there and save ourselves some money." I wanted to make the venture sound as low-risk as possible. "Of course, Howard," I went on, "We don't process the credit-card receipts, and we send everyone a premium for their trouble."

He was horrified. I knew this because he rolled out from behind his computer.

"There is absolutely no way that I can agree to that, Peter. But thank you." End of conversation.

Back in my office, I shut the door and called Randee.

"He didn't go for it," I told her glumly.

"What did he say?"

"He just said no. I think he was scared of becoming a manufacturer, of warehousing product and processing receipts from customers. That's a whole different business for him."

Howard and Alan were studio guys. Howard's business was built upon the fact that Alan fished up a hot social topic, dressed it up with a writer and director, and then pitched it to a network. The network guys said, "Here's $3 million, as long as you can get so-and-so to star. The thing aired twice. Then Howard would sell it into syndication or sell it abroad. It was a nice business, a clean business. They needed infomercials like a hole in the head.

"I don't think it helped to mention a dry test," I continued. "The idea of advertising a product on television without actually having made the product. . . . Geez, what was I thinking?"

In my desperation to win Howard's approval, I'd tried to sell a practice that he properly rejected. I reject it now, too, as does NIMA and most companies in the field.

"Well, it was a good shot," she said, trying to sound encouraging. But she sounded tired. I told her I had to get going, that I had a meeting.

I didn't.

The following week, Randee and I were having dinner at this little Tuscan place we like. It's next to Randee's favorite antique store, so she can browse before dinner. I like their desserts. Anything gooey and rich, that's for me.

"Randee," I said, snapping a breadstick, "I want to quit Landsburg. Howard said no to an infomercial, so the videos are gonna go nowhere. Besides, what's really exciting to me *are* the infomercials. I mean, why should I be a video producer with a marketing problem when I can be an infomercial producer and sell whatever I want?" (The moment I'd thought of this, just hours earlier, my spirits rose.)

"Well, what would you sell?" she asked, mopping up olive oil with a piece of bread.

"Doesn't matter. Anything." I snapped another breadstick.

"Anything," she repeated. She looked worried.

To ease her mind, I told her I'd negotiate an extension of my contract with Landsburg while I looked for a potential investor for my new venture.

I called Charles Silverberg, a snazzy L.A. lawyer whose client list included Jessica Lange, Donald Sutherland—a slew of stars. I asked him to negotiate my contract with Landsburg. I also mentioned that I thought the future lay in infomercials, not special-interest video, and secretly hoped that I'd get a break before I had to sign another Landsburg contract.

My presentation to investors would include industry anecdotes, some history, and facts and figures. I started calling people in the business, anyone who'd talk to me, to gather material. I kept my ears perked for colorful stories; I wanted to sound like an expert and also be entertaining. It makes for a stronger presentation.

I knew that short-form infomercials had been around for years—who could forget the spots for Ron Popeil's Veg-O-Matic and Pocket Fisherman? But long-form infomercials were something new. To my surprise, however, *Everybody's Money Matters* wasn't the first one. That, I learned, was an inspired accident.

In 1982, a talk show aired on a local cable access station in San Diego. The show revolved around a hair regeneration product. People liked the show, called *New Generation,* which was the name of the product, so the inventor contacted the Chicago-based A. Eicoff & Company to buy air time on other broadcast stations. Frank Cannella, an aggressive young account supervisor at Eicoff who now heads Cannella Response Television, looked at the tape, tacked on an 800 number, and started calling up program directors to see if they'd air it. He pitched the show as no different than paid religious programming. Cannella didn't realize that the Sunday morning television preachers had the blessing of the Federal Communications Commission, while "program-length commercials," as the early infomercials were called, did not. (Hey, he was a kid.) Still, many stations accepted the program—it *was* a talk show, after all—and the FCC never said a word.

Meanwhile, things were percolating in the most unlikely of places, Fairfield, Iowa.

Maharishi International University had opened in Fairfield in 1974, and, over the next 10 years, hundreds of practitioners of transcendental meditation from across the country arrived to meditate together in domes. One of them was Ed Beckley.

Beckley, a tall, skinny man with a high-pitched voice and a bumpkin stage persona held seminars in hotel meeting rooms, where he preached a method of buying real estate with "no money down," that is, cutting deals with the desperate owners of distressed properties. It was the same get-rich-quick scheme you heard about on Tony's show; a lot of guys peddled it in the '80s. Beckley charged up to $500 for the live seminar and made a nice piece of change from the books and tapes he sold to the converted when it was over.

He'd been airing a "documentary" about financial wealth on television that, at the end, urged people to attend his live seminars. Then, in the fall of 1984, he got the idea to produce an infomercial with an 800 number, so people could purchase his books and tapes over the phone with their credit cards. The company took off. Within 12 months, The Beckley Group grew from 25 to 550 employees.

Goodbye Holiday Inns! Hello beach house in Maui!

Beckley hired Tim Hawthorne to oversee the infomercial campaign. Hawthorne is now chairman of Hawthorne Communications in Fairfield, whose clients include Time-Life, Apple, and Nissan. Hawthorne, like Beckley, practiced TM—he still does—and moved to Fairfield to be close to other meditators. He hired Katie Williams to open a separate division devoted to infomercials. She now heads Williams Television Time in Los Angeles, one of the biggest media-buying agencies in the infomercial industry. The Maharishi failed to bring world peace, but he paved the way for the MicroCrisp!

In 1985, Hawthorne purchased a block of six hours on the Discovery Channel for Beckley's *Millionaire Maker.* The show aired in half-hour slots between 3 A.M. and 9 A.M. The cost of each half hour was $50.

The reason overnight media time was so cheap was because no one wanted it. Buying media time, say, on a UHF channel frequently meant asking the station manager how much it would cost to keep the engineer around and the transmitter on after the regular programming was over. (Things have changed. Infomercials are a major revenue source for most TV stations and cable networks. With their rise in popularity, media prices have risen 500 percent on average and, in some venues, 5,000 percent.)

The more I learned about the infomercial business, the more I liked it. After speaking with more than a dozen people in the industry (I'm still amazed that these folks consented to talk with a stranger—and talked at length), I spent the next week in the library at the USC School of Business. I knew I needed to wow potential investors with my knowledge of infomercials, so I rolled up my sleeves and dived into trade publications and other sources of industry information. But after a few days, my enthusiasm waned. I began to feel ridiculous. Here I was, sitting in a cubicle, surrounded by people twenty years younger than me, boning up on an industry I knew nothing about.

I'm too old for this. The odds are stacked against me. I'm wasting my time.

But I ploughed on and finished writing a presentation. I got to use it a few days later.

A mutual friend introduced me to a fellow named Jack Parks,* who had money to invest. Great! Parks lived in the Ahwatukee neighborhood in Phoenix and had made some serious money in the oil business. After exchanging phone calls, we decided to meet. I asked Randee to go with me. We'd make it our final fling before the baby came. She started packing.

I'd found an investor. I was off and running.

We checked into the hotel. It was actually a resort, but it was nondescript. There was a pool, a golf course, and acres of beige carpet. After hanging up our clothes, we headed for Parks' house in our rental car. As usual, I got lost. We stopped twice for directions. Finally we found his street. Big homes. A good sign, I

---

* Jack Parks is a pseudonym.

thought. Randee started counting the house numbers. They were descending. Ah. Here it was. We pulled into the driveway.

"Here goes nothing!" I said as we climbed out of the car.

Parks greeted us warmly and invited us into his living room. Right away I could tell something was wrong. There was nowhere to sit. I don't mean the room was sparsely furnished—I'm not talking about a preference for minimalism—I mean it looked like he'd been robbed.

Randee claimed the one chair she could find. I lied that I felt stiff from the plane ride and that I preferred to stand.

After talking about the weather, which, in Phoenix, means talking about the heat, we got down to business. Then the door bell rang.

"Excuse me," said Parks, jumping up. There was a family at the door. A husband, a wife, two kids. They stood in the entrance hall and chatted with him. On their way upstairs, they shot a glance at the living room.

I looked at Randee. She looked at the ceiling.

Parks returned and we resumed our conversation.

A few minutes later the doorbell rang again. He excused himself once more. This time, it was a young couple. At this rate we'd be here till dinner. It was ten o'clock in the morning.

The interruptions were getting hard to ignore. So I asked Jack if he was selling his house. He explained that his wife had served him papers and he had to dump the property quickly, even though it was a down market. I asked him where he was planning to move and he said into a studio apartment because the divorce had bled him.

Randee shot me a look. She knew how I'd tried to peddle film packages. She was there when I pitched the limited partnership to produce videos. In other words, she knew about dead ends. *So,* her eyes seemed to say, *how come you didn't do your homework?* I looked the other way.

Ever resourceful, she feigned fatigue. We shook hands with Parks, promised to be in touch, and got the hell out of there. On the drive back to the hotel, we stared straight ahead. We barely spoke.

Back in the room, I got ready to go to the baseball game. Park's partner couldn't meet with us in the morning, so he'd invited me to a spring training game, the Angels versus the Brewers. Randee would spend the afternoon at the zoo with the guy's wife. I took my shirt and tie off.

"You're still gonna go to the game?" she asked sharply.

"I can't cancel now. It wouldn't be right." (Actually, I wanted to go. I'd never been to a spring training game. A major league game in a small stadium!)

She glowered.

"Look, I have to go." I started tying my Reeboks.

"What about us? I thought this weekend was gonna be romantic. 'Our last fling before the baby,' you said."

"Well, we have tomorrow."

"No, we don't. We're leaving at one o'clock."

"We'll have a nice brunch."

"*You'll* have a nice brunch." With that, she walked out and slammed the door. Seconds later she marched back in, grabbed her bathing suit, and slammed the door again. I gathered she wasn't going to the zoo.

I ran after her. By the time we got to the pool, we were shouting at each other about ball games and zoo trips. If we'd been honest, we would have admitted how frightened we were and probably fallen into each other's arms. But no, we fought. Dumb. Finally I threw the room key on her lounge chair and stomped back to the room.

I dropped onto the bed, bouncing Randee's toiletries bag to the floor. I leaned over and picked it up, then threw it down again. I hoped I broke something.

How could I be so stupid? I never should have come down here. I *hadn't* done my homework. My dream of starting a business had crashed and burned.

I reached for the remote and clicked on the TV. On one of the cable stations was an infomercial.

CHAPTER · 2

Hat in Hand

When the weekend came, Randee and I drove to Venice beach. We'd made up, but I wasn't any happier. All I could think about was how I'd failed to get my business off the ground. Randee thought a trip to Venice might cheer me up.

The town is known principally for its beach and its gangs. But in the '50s and '60s, it was home to the beatniks, whose heroes included Allen Ginsberg, William Burroughs, and Jack Kerouac. The beats spent a lot of time in smoke-filled coffeehouses listening to bad poetry and bad-mouthing the bourgeoisie. They vehemently rejected the shackles of middle-class life forged during the Eisenhower years and deplored the mass of lives led in quiet desperation, to paraphrase Thoreau, that 19th-century beat.

The beats and the coffeehouses are gone now, but the noncon-formist spirit is alive and well in Venice.

Though a wide, inviting stretch of sand well-attended by sea-gulls, the beach is more famous for its weirdness and bodacious roller-bladers than its natural beauty. Cross a Middle Eastern bazaar with the Atlantic City boardwalk, add a pinch of the East Village, and you've got it. The way I see it, why waste time dozing in the sun when there's so much to see? It's the perfect beach for people who hate to go to the beach. People like me.

All our favorites were there: the self-proclaimed World's Greatest Wino (he's a panhandler); the roller-blading Rastafarian with his electric guitar (it's painted red, white, and blue); the cheerful, if toasted, men and women who build elaborate sand sculptures all day long; yet another earnest young girl selling homemade candles (Does the city hand out kits to these kids when they get off the bus from Dubuque?); and, my hero, the gray-haired, bandana-headed palmist whose sign reads: NO CHARGE. JUST PAY WHAT YOU FEEL THE READING DESERVES. It doesn't get any groovier than this.

While I watched the parade of tourists on the sidewalk, Randee browsed through the kiosks crammed with batik scarves and tie-dyed shirts, belts studded with tiny bells, and those stiff leather bracelets. Even now, she's partial to long, cotton skirts and loose blouses. Rodeo Drive holds no charm for her.

Me? I'm a polo-shirt-and-chinos guy. Venice beach doesn't cater to my crowd.

It was almost noon when we decided to go for lunch. We chose The Rose Cafe; the food's good, and across the street is an ice cream parlor where I like to go for dessert. The ice cream parlor is one of the city's official traffic schools. No kidding. There's a sign over the door, TRAFFIC SCHOOL FOR CHOCOHOLICS. If you get a ticket you can choose to take a course here to keep your driving record clean and prevent your insurance from going up, though not your cholesterol level. (This is California. We handle things a bit differently here, including penalties for moving violations.)

I got myself a chocolate raspberry. Randee abstained. We strolled along the sidewalk, past the public basketball court where some of the best pick-up games in the country can be seen, past Muscle Beach (yes, *the* Muscle Beach), which is really an outdoor gym. Seeing the body-builders only made me think about the Weider exercise video, how it would languish on the shelf now that Howard had nixed the infomercial.

"C'mon," I said somberly. "Let's turn around."

Randee didn't budge. "It's getting to you," she said gently.

I shrugged. "Jack Parks and his partner were all I had." I started to walk away.

She came around in front of me. She spoke very quietly. "Remember when I turned in the first draft of the Paramount script and they hated it?"

"Yeah," I said, recalling her disappointment. She'd had second thoughts about being a screenwriter. But she hung in there and things turned around.

"And remember how you gave me that great speech about being lost on a country road at night? You're following somebody's directions, looking for a white farmhouse, and you drive and drive until you start thinking you must have passed it in the dark. It *can't* be this far. You turn back, only to find out that the house you were looking for was just a half mile past where you gave up."

She touched my hand. "Remember that speech? Give that speech to yourself," she said.

She was right. The analogy applied to my situation then, because just like driving at night, starting a business is guaranteed to make you feel lost and confused. It doesn't mean you *are* lost and confused. But if you let those feelings undermine your confidence, you may abandon a winning project just before it turns the corner. So, trust the directions. Stick with your plan.

If Randee raised my spirits, Charles Silverberg, my lawyer, sent them into orbit. He surprised me with a call, and he had terrific news. "I've got a client who may be willing to bankroll your venture," he said. "She's interested in direct-response advertising.

She's an actress, but she's best-known for her association with Lorimar. Her name is Pippa Scott."

I didn't recognize the name. "What's she been in?"

"Older stuff. *Auntie Mame. The Searchers.*"

The Searchers. Wow! The great John Ford classic! Maybe the best Western ever made. In film school it's analyzed backward and forward. John Wayne plays a Civil War veteran whose brother's family is murdered by Indians, but one child is spared, abducted, and raised as a squaw. The Duke spends years trying to find her. When he does, his niece is all grown up—and she's Natalie Wood. But there's an unexpected twist, rare in the genre. She refuses to leave the tribe.

Pippa Scott played the family's eldest daughter. She's setting the table for dinner when the family learns that the savages are thundering toward their cabin. Anticipating the horror of her death, she screams. (There's a saying in film school: "If you write it right, you don't have to show the Indians.") The camera zooms in for a close-up of her terrified face. Alfred Hitchcock and John Carpenter—not to mention Macaulay Culkin—owe a lot to that scream.

Pippa's father, Allan Scott, was a Hollywood screenwriter. He wrote or collaborated on the screenplays for Fred Astaire and Ginger Rogers musicals—*Top Hat, Swing Time, Shall We Dance,* and others. When Pippa was a little girl, she watched Astaire and his choreographer Hermes Pan rehearse at the old RKO Studios. Then Ginger Rogers would show up, and she and Fred would rehearse. Pippa knew lots of stars growing up.

She became one herself. Not a big star, mind you, but she had a decent career. She played the young decorator the nephew marries in *Auntie Mame,* starring Rosalind Russell, and had a role in *Petulia,* starring George C. Scott and Julie Christie, a classic '60s film, now a cult favorite. She did a lot of TV; she played the newspaper publisher Molly Wood on the long-running NBC show *The Virginian.*

But she is best known, at least in the film business, for her association with Lorimar Productions, which produced *Dallas, Knots Landing, Falcon Crest,* and a host of other successful television programs. Her ex-husband, Lee Rich, a former advertising executive, founded Lorimar with Merv Adelson in 1969. The project that launched Lorimar was *The Homecoming,* the TV movie that gave birth to *The Waltons* television series. It was Pippa who found the script. She knew the writer, Earl Hammer. They were friends.

When she divorced Rich in 1983, she received in settlement an 11 percent stock interest in Lorimar—worth roughly $18 million at the time of the split-up, according to *Forbes.* Three years later, she sold a big part of her stake back to Adelson just as the shares reached a peak of 33.

Pippa Scott was loaded.

I called her immediately. We set up a meeting.

Her office was on Wilshire Boulevard in Westwood, a commercial area dominated by UCLA but not without some charm. A few years earlier, Pippa had launched her own film company, Linden Productions. She had been married to a powerful man and, though it's just my opinion, may have wanted to prove herself capable of succeeding on her own. Lucky for her, she had more than enough money to try. And she knew the film business.

Her goal was to make low-budget, high-quality feature films. When I contacted her, she was trying to make a movie called *Hunting Cockroaches* that was based on an off-broadway play starring Dianne Wiest and Ron Silver. It was a comedy written by Polish writer Janusz Glowacki; the *New York Times'* Frank Rich had pronounced the play "brash" and "delightful." Anyway, she'd managed to interest William Hurt, the actor, and Sidney Lumet, the director. But each had a window of availability, and naturally those windows were open at different times. That's how it goes in Hollywood. Independent feature companies try to package a script with a star and a director and sell the project to the studios, but getting the package together is tricky business. It's hard to get a commitment from the big names the studios want and hard to keep those commitments alive. It's like juggling. Just when you think you've got all the balls in the air, one of 'em drops with a thud.

She had not had a great deal of success, so she was looking at other business opportunities. She was considering starting a talent agency or maybe a foreign-film distribution company. My timing was excellent.

Pippa's office space wasn't anything like Landsburg's. The walls were a crisp white—the carpet was thick and a merry green. Sunlight poured through the windows. French doors opened into the conference room, and another pair opened into Pippa's executive suite—a feminine touch. The plants were thriving. The whole office was like a solarium in some splendid home in *Architectural Digest*. But the best thing was the art. After her divorce, she bought fabulous paintings. She spent with abandon. Like a curator, she would circulate them through the office. She often asked me what I preferred.

But I'm getting ahead of myself.

When I arrived at Pippa's office, I waited on an antique bench in the reception area and stared at a poster on the wall. It was for a movie released months earlier called *Meet the Hollowheads,* a dark comedy about the future where life is sustained by a vast system of tubes and giant worms are the food supply. *Yuck.* Why would Pippa Scott hang such a thing in her office? (Simple. She'd produced it.)

After a few minutes, her personal secretary Hillary showed me to an oversized white couch in Pippa's executive suite. I moved the white pillows aside and sat down. On the coffee table was a bottle of Evian but no glasses. A man appeared in the doorway and introduced himself as Joe Grace. His job was to read the spreadsheets, "to watch the bottom line," he explained, taking a seat on the couch. He told me that, before teaming up with Pippa, he'd worked for Arnon Milchan. Milchan is a major player in Hollywood, a real mogul. He's produced *The War of the Roses, Pretty Woman,* and *Under Siege,* to name a few films, and he's been widely reported to have been an arms dealer for Israel. Regardless of the occasion, from an awards show to a bar mitzvah, Milchan wears a white T-shirt and pants. Joe had adopted the uniform.

We chatted for a minute, then Pippa burst in, apologizing for keeping us waiting.

She was charming and gracious. Attractive, too. Red hair, blue eyes. A softer, prettier Lucille Ball. She had excellent diction. I liked her instantly.

What appealed to her about direct-response television, she said, was that she believed infomercials presented an attractive opportunity for investment. Given her background in film, why not get in on the ground floor of a hot new industry?

Great. The conversation was headed in the direction I wanted to take it—the big picture. I had a severe liability in this meeting. When you're pitching an investor, you usually start out with a litany of your past successes to establish your credibility and bolster their confidence in you. But I had no track record in infomercials whatsoever. What I did have was a lot of research about an industry that was new, fast-growing, profitable, and exciting. And that's where I started.

I mentioned some of the big successes of the day—*Mindpower,* written by my new friend Jim McNamara, which had grossed over $65 million. And *Arnold Morris' Great Wok of China,* with sales of over $36 million.

I sketched out the reasons for the explosive growth of the business. The Federal Communications Commission was responsible for two of them: the deregulation of commercial time and the decision in the early '80s to accelerate approval of new broadcasting licenses. There were 1,411 TV stations in the country, I told her, up 40 percent from the early '80s. That was a big increase in the most precious commodity in the TV direct response business: broadcast time. And cable was growing equally rapidly. Sixty percent of TV households were wired for cable, up from only 23 percent in 1980. New cable networks like Nostalgia and the Nashville Network were coming online to keep company with the pioneers like ESPN and CNN.

I touched on the importance of remote controls (infomercials are designed to grab channel-surfers) and threw in a bit about the proliferation of credit cards in the late '70s and early '80s.

Then I tried to explain why infomercials are so appealing. One reason is people like to shop when they're relaxed. And where are they more relaxed than at home? Infomercials work for exactly the same reason that door-to-door sales calls work: The audience is receptive. Anyone who invites you into their home and gives you the time to explain your product so it really makes sense, the time to offer encouragement and to respond to likely questions—to just plain entertain—is a potential buyer.

Pippa and Joe probably knew a lot of this already, having done their own research. Joe's next question confirmed this. He cut to the chase: "Let's talk about market testing." (Testing is one of the most attractive features of direct response from an investment point of view because it reduces risk. He was right to bring it up.)

"Okay. No other marketing strategy lends itself better to fast, accurate testing because you're talking directly to your customers nationwide. Eighty percent of the orders will come by phone, and they'll all come into the same inbound telephone marketing operation, where they're immediately entered into a database. This database provides overnight comparisons between the sales figures from different versions of our infomercial running in different cities to tell us what is working with consumers."

I kept going.

"For example, if we want to test price points, we run infomercials in demographically similar cities. The infomercials are identical except for the price. Overnight, we begin comparing sales volume and gross revenues from each market to decide which price point is the most profitable. Once we know the best price, we run through the other elements, including consumer promise, visuals, and so on."

Pippa leaned forward.

"The media plan itself will also be tested by varying the time of day, market demographics, cable versus broadcast, and so forth. Certain successful results may call for retesting. For instance, if we change the sales pitch to broaden the appeal, we may want to take another look at price. All of this can be done quickly and inexpensively by shooting extra footage on the set and varying the voice-over narration. When we're done, we have an infomercial that has proven its ability to produce sales and profits at a predictable rate. This is the one we buy time for and broadcast across the country, on cable networks and station-by-station in a nation-wide roll-out."

"It's like the theater," said Pippa, turning to Joe. "You open in Toronto or Boston, work out the kinks, then bring the show to Broadway."

"Exactly," I said. She smiled.

So far, I had pitched the profitability and growth of the industry and the ways that testing could limit risk—in other words, the reasons why people already in the business had gotten into it and how they played the game. Now I wanted to give Pippa a reason to back me over anyone else with a desire to break in. So I explained how I would build a different kind of company. It started with the hundreds of millions of dollars the industry left on the table every year by overlooking a major source of revenue that was theirs for the asking—retail.

I asked Pippa if she had ever bought anything off television. She shook her head. "I'm not surprised," I said. "I haven't either. Even if I like a product, I won't pick up the phone and order it. I want to hold something before I buy it. And I think most people are like us. Problem is, most successful TV products never make it into stores. When the TV campaign is over, the product disappears. You spend all that money advertising a product, but you never make it available where most people do all of their shopping—in a store. What a waste."

They looked puzzled. They didn't see where I was headed.

"There are two reasons for this," I continued. "First, people in direct response are scared of retail. Too many headaches, they think. And second, a lot of TV products wouldn't withstand retail scrutiny. Sure, they look good on TV, but up close and personal?—forget it. They're shoddy. So, our first challenge is to find a good product, a product that *retail* customers will be willing to buy."

"You're saying you want to go retail?" asked Joe.

Yes, I said. "When we have a successful campaign, we're going to spend $5 million to $10 million on a media blitz. All out of cash flow. Everybody in America is going to be aware of our product and its benefits. We're going to have a recognizable brand name that store shoppers will be asking for. Let's make sure we have product on the shelves for them to buy."

"What about the headaches?" Joe asked. "From what I understand, it's not that easy to get the big chains to give shelf space to a new product."

"That's true," I said. I told him how only a small number of truly new products make it on to store shelves and how these products are introduced by very large corporations or by indefatigable entrepreneurs who knock on the store chain doors for years before they're allowed in. "But an infomercial campaign allows us to bypass that tedious process. With a good ad, supported by millions of dollars in media, we'll be way ahead of most small entrepreneurs who have little or no advertising. Customers will be walking into stores demanding our product. Store buyers will have no choice but to stock the item."

I turned to Pippa.

"And after it's on the store shelves, I want everyone in the country to be talking about it. Fads have happened before but by accident—the Hula Hoop, the Mood Ring. But with direct response, Pippa, we can create the momentum that ignites the fad. Retail's the goal; fad status, the icing on the cake."

"You're talking about explosive growth," said Joe.

"Yes, I am. It's a big challenge. You're selling 2 million units within ten months, not over five years. You have to make them, box them, store them, and ship them."

"How would you manage it? Finance it?" he asked.

"By building a core company that handles product development and marketing but outsources manufacturing, warehousing, credit card processing, telemarketing, and so on."

Blank stares. I searched my mind for an analogy. The movies!

"The model for this kind of company has been around for a long, long time, and in fact is the kind of company you're most familiar with, Pippa: a Hollywood production company. Take Landsburg. It employs about two dozen people on a permanent basis. Everyone else is on contract. When they're making a movie for television, when they're 'in production,' the number of people employed tops one hundred fifty. When it's a wrap, the number shrinks back down to the permanent staff. There's a constant ebb and flow. It's the same with an infomercial company."

With one important difference, though. The average $35,000 two-minute, short-form infomercial is a pretty basic production. One step up from a slide show. Marketing expertise, not production experience, is the essential ingredient for success. More often than not, I told her, products failed to sell not because they were bad products but because they were poorly marketed—at least, that was my analysis.

Pippa took a swig from the Evian bottle. Then she leaned back in her chair and folded her arms. "Well, what's your product?"

"The company's expertise will be marketing," I said, sidestepping the question. "Believe me, inventors will flock to us."

She rubbed her earlobe. There was an awkward silence.

"Well," I said, clearing my throat, "I did come across something interesting on a trip to Phoenix . . ." Jack Parks had told me about an Israeli product, a spray someone had shown him. A few spritzes and it lowered the temperature inside your car on a hot day. I thought it sounded neat.

"I don't want to do crap," she shot back. She was all Hollywood, all right.

"I don't either," I assured her. "Crap won't get us into Wal-Mart. It's just an example."

She ran her fingers through her hair.

Here it comes, I thought. I braced myself—*Peter, you have no track record in the infomercial business. How can you possibly pull this off?* But, to my surprise, she didn't bring it up. She didn't even ask why I felt qualified to choose a manufacturer. My strategy worked: I'd succeeded in pitching the industry.

Finally we got around to my business plan, which was simple. Be ready for failures and be ready to take successes retail. I told Pippa that the company's first order of business was to find products, produce shows, and test them. And I wanted her to look at this production slate as the company's research and development program, because even the guys who've been doing this for years failed most of the time. It's just like the movie business. One hit pays for a lot of flops.

I said I hoped that the first infomercial would be successful and make the company self-sustaining right off the bat, but that we had to be prepared to suffer a number of failures and write-offs before we got it right. I used investing in stocks as an analogy. Buying one stock is a gamble, buying eight stocks is an investment plan. I told her she had to be prepared to finance eight infomercial productions and tests. I was confident that in eight I could find one hit.

She took another swig of water. "How much money do you need?"

"Well, I suppose, if you figure in the legal fees; the licensing fees; the cost of producing eight shows, script through final editing; my salary—I'd say, oh, $750,000. That's assuming seven flops, of course. My hope is that number 2 is the hit, not number 8."

She got up and walked to the window, her back turned toward us. She lingered there a moment, the sun causing her red hair to glint. She whirled around. "We'll be in touch, Peter. It's been a pleasure meeting with you. Gotta run. I'm late for lunch."

I just sat there. I had no idea if I'd just spent the last forty minutes wasting my time or if I'd made an impression. Until we'd talked money, she seemed enthusiastic. Now she wore a poker face. Joe stood up, so I stood up. Pippa extended her hand. I shook it, then I shook Joe's.

Time to go home and wait by the phone.

Before leaving her office, I made a call. Shortly afterward, while walking to my car, I saw her pull out of the parking lot driving a Jeep with a custom paint job in British racing green. No limo. No driver. I liked that.

Two kinds of start-up entrepreneurs try infomercial marketing: small investors, often inventors, with a kitty of $15,000 to $30,000 to spend on a single low-budget infomercial; and businesspeople with access to more significant start-up funding who improve the odds by investing in a number of infomercials at once. Either way, the information in this book can help you. But I feel compelled to say a few words about the size of the investment needed to pursue the latter course, since that's the route I took.

Knowing what I know now, I'd have to say that $750,000 was high for a start-up company. I think you could have a very good shot at this business for $250,000. Here's how it would break down.

First of all, you'd decide to do short-form only. Short-form infomercials run under two minutes. Long-form infomercials always run 28½ minutes, and they cost a lot more to produce. Second, you'd go the noncelebrity route. The majority of short-form infomercials don't use celebrities. Third, you'd budget for five shows, because with this book in hand your odds improve. And the products you'd choose would be *products*—that is, *things*—not self-improvement or diet programs. Product infomercials, which are usually demonstration shows, are the cheapest to make. And when they work, their grosses equal or surpass those of shows that cost more to produce. The Contour Pillow ad grossed tens of millions of dollars and cost less than $25,000 to produce.

You'd spend $30,000 per show for five shows. That's $150,000. You'd then need to put aside money for legal fees because you have to acquire the rights to these products. (I'm assuming you're not an inventor.) I'd put aside $15,000 for legal fees. And don't advance more than $5,000 to acquire the rights for each product. Then you've got to pay for a test, and that will run you about $5,000 per show, which leaves $35,000 for everything else. I'm assuming you wouldn't be drawing a salary, which, incidentally, would not be unusual. Most entrepreneurs starting a company do not pay themselves a salary, at least not during the development phase. This would get you through the testing process. Where you go from there, well, that comes later.

Compared to other entrepreneurial opportunities, infomercials are a conservative bet. Why? Well, if you put $250,000 into a restaurant, which is the obvious start-up, or say, a retail store, you've got one shot. If it doesn't work, if you choose the wrong menu or the wrong location, you're out the $250,000. With infomercials, you've got five chances to strike it rich. (And I do mean rich. The return is far greater than with a restaurant or a boutique. You're not going to turn $250,000 into $40 million with Harry's Hat Emporium.)

But before you put that $40 million in the bank, you've got to have made some right choices. Here are six questions to ask yourself:

1. *Is your product right for direct response?* Does it demonstrate well? If it's a service, is it going to have repeat business?
2. *Should you shoot a short-form or long-form infomercial?* One and two minute or 30 minutes? The decision should be based on your price point, the complexity of your product, and your plans to go retail.
3. *If you go with long-form, what format do you choose?* Newsmagazine dominated by location reports; talk show with a host and guests; storymercial with a story line and characters; demonstration show; seminar with a speaker and an audience.
4. *Does your copy strategy work?* What compelling promise can you make about using the product that will make people want to buy it? Don't leave this to your copywriter. You know the product better than anyone.
5. *Are you casting the right spokesperson?* Celebrity or non-celebrity, male or female, young or old. The wrong celebrity is worse than no celebrity at all.
6. *Is your offer effective?* Have you looked closely at your payment plan, guarantee, price point, and premiums?

I'll return to this list in greater detail throughout the book.
Back to Pippa.

The following week Joe called me in Canada. I was visiting family. I hung up and winked at Randee. "I got the money," I said. She grinned, touching her wedding ring, our code for "Yes!" because that's the inscription on the inside of our rings. She was seven months pregnant. She sure looked relieved.

Why did Pippa go for it? I honestly don't know. Perhaps I painted a vision that caught her fancy. Perhaps she was looking for something she could point to and say, "I made it happen." There's a deep satisfaction in that. You don't get it from investing in stocks or bonds or real estate where the rewards are strictly financial. On the other hand, backing a start-up is more complicated because you're not simply risking your money. You're risking your reputation as a businessperson. Should the venture fail—and most start-ups do—you may feel duped, like waking up in the morning with a hangover and finding your wallet's gone. Investors like the *idea* of financing a dream, but they rarely commit. Whatever her reason, Pippa took a chance on a stranger and that took guts.

The first thing I did when we returned to L.A. was move into Pippa's offices. (Alan and Howard bid me a fond farewell, though I doubt they were sorry to see me go.) I took an empty office at the back and brought my assistant, Leslie Friedberg, with me.

After we hung Pippa's paintings on the walls (she'd juxtaposed a Japanese-influenced abstract with a superrealist English landscape to great effect), I sharpened some pencils and sat down to study the business plan. Flipping through the pages, it hit me—I gotta deliver on this. More specifically, I needed to have three shows testing within six months. Yikes!

I took a deep breath. That part of the plan looked overly ambitious. Luckily, other parts seemed more realistic and doable. For one thing, I'd planned for a small, core company. Looking back, I'm glad that I did.

A direct-response company needs the structure of a virtual corporation. I can't say this enough. Such a structure allows the company to expand and contract at will. This is important because the growth curve of a TV-promoted fad has a steep rise and then a gradual fall. At the end of a campaign, you want to end up with cash, access to retail shelves, and a hot reputation to ensure that inventors will bring you more products.

The danger of a direct-response hit is failing to recognize this. It's folly to build a vertically integrated company, to buy warehouses and a factory—to do all the things one assumes one should do when you have a hot product. Direct response is a different animal. Cash is king. You move on to the next product, the next campaign.

51

So I'd stick with a virtual structure. Everything would be out-sourced except the company's core functions: marketing, distribution, and product acquisition. Revenues, not assets, would be the yardstick for success.

The first thing I did was hire an attorney to handle contracts—for the rights to products, for fulfillment, and for telemarketing. Actually, that was the second thing I did; the first thing was to name the company. Well, Leslie did. She also named Holly. What can I say?—she had a knack.

While Ovation took shape, I conducted research: I watched television. *Hours and hours of television.* I began to see what made infomercials so compelling. They responded to deeply felt, almost chronic needs. To look and feel better. To make more money. To spend less time cooking and cleaning. There was a "gotta have it" aspect to the products. The reason was simple: *a product that appeals to an aching need results in impulse buying.*

So, who were the people watching and buying? Judging by the infomercials, they weren't pikers. They had well-equipped kitchens, patios with barbecues, rec rooms, backyards. They had draperies that needed steam cleaning, silver flatware to keep from tarnishing. They had cars. They owned homes.

They looked to be middle class.

They were. And they are.

According to a 1995 Leisure Trends Gallup poll conducted for the National Infomercial Marketing Association (NIMA), 29 percent of the general population over the age of 16 has an annual income of $20,000 to $40,000. These middle-class Americans are heavy buyers of direct-response television products, representing 34 percent of the industry's customers. The balance of DRTV buyers breaks down along the lines of the general population—23 percent of DRTV buyers make $60,000-plus, compared with 21 percent of the general population; 17 percent make $40,000 to $60,000, compared with 19 percent of the general population; and 16 percent make less than $20,000, compared with 18 percent of the general population. (These numbers don't add up to 100 because of people who responded "don't know" or refused to respond.)

They're not waiting to win the lottery. They're people with disposable income.

Yet I was right to assume they weren't *wealthy*. Pippa lobbied for high-end merchandise—at one point, a gourmet cooking system. It included little bottles with the ingredients for Dijon chicken, beef Wellington, and Peking duck, as I recall. I told her our audience was more interested in hamburgers and spaghetti. These people had kids. "Do me a favor. The next time you're flying into New York, look down at the rows of houses on Long Island. *That's our crowd.*"

"You mean the ones with the above-ground pools?" she asked innocently. I held my tongue.

But back to the tube.

The more infomercials I watched, the more I learned. I found *Amazing Discoveries* hosted by Mike Levey particularly instructive.

Amazing Discoveries billed itself as "dedicated to new products and new ideas that make your life easier and more enjoyable." Levey, producer and host, played the straight man to wacky guests with indispensable products like Auri car wax (his guest set a car on fire) and the Europainter. (His current show, *Ask Mike,* has the same format. Levey is a multimillionaire who in 1995 merged his company, Positive Response Television, with National Media in a deal worth a reported $26 million.)

Levey was less a host than a pal. Wearing glasses and a sweater, he looked like one of your goofy friends from college. An amiable nerd—with a microphone. He seemed to discover the products along with the TV audience, exclaiming "Wow!" and "Isn't that amazing!" as though he'd never seen them before. His Europainter infomercial was the first *Amazing Discoveries* show I ever saw. It taught me the value of a good demonstration.

Levey's guest was Ian Long, who he said came "all the way from England to show us the Europainter." Indeed, Long had what sounded like a Cockney accent. There were quaint references to "skirting boards" (baseboards) and "English-type wallpaper." The product was a kind of synthetic sponge that soaked up paint but didn't drip or spatter. There were different-sized sponges for different jobs. It would save you time, save you paint, and most important, save you money.

But what was more "amazing" than the product was Long's performance. He painted walls, baseboards, window sills, ceilings, chairs, rough cedar shingles. He moved swiftly from one set to the next, from one prop to the next. He never fumbled, never missed his mark. The subliminal message was, "This product won't fail you."

He got Levey involved, too. He put a Europainter in his hand and told him to paint a brick wall that just happened to be there. "Ian, look. I'm doing this! It's easy!" cried Mike, boyishly.

Long asked three people from the audience to come up on stage. He attached a broom handle to the end of the Europainter and shook it at them. They flinched. "No roller spatter whatsoever," he beamed. The audience cheered. He proceeded to paint the bit of ceiling over the trio's heads. Still no drips. The audience clapped wildly. The entertainment value of the demonstration was obvious. It was like a magic trick.

But something else was going on. There was an immediacy to the show that was palpable. A cameraman ran in front of Long while he was doing his demonstration, unheard of in taped television. Levey himself walked right in front of a camera. And in a shot of the three people Long had plucked from the audience, you could see a guy with a hand-held camera crouching on the ground.

Mistakes? Hardly.

Amazing Discoveries had the look and feel of the early days of television—live and unrehearsed—but it was neither. It was choreographed. (Several years later a long-time producer of the show told me Levey rehearsed for *four days* before going to tape.) Levey and his team worked hard to conjure a feeling of spontaneity, because the more unrehearsed the demonstration looked, the more credible the product would appear to the television audience. (Remember the live Alpo spots on *The Tonight Show?* Very effective.)

But where would I find products like the Europainter system, not to mention an experienced pitchman like Ian Long? Easy, I thought. The home shows, the garden shows, the county and state fairs. I started traveling around the country. Pippa often joined me. It was a lark for her. The fairs were great theater.

Outside, the barkers hurled their come-ons at us ("You win every time," "Cheap, family fun, that's how it's done"). Inside, in the exhibition halls, we were assaulted by the most aggressive odors—fried dough, hot pizza, cotton candy, sweet perfume. There were young women pushing strollers, their babies clutching Yosemite Sams and Porky Pigs, booty from the dime toss or dart games; beefy men with tattooed arms eyeing water purification systems and car alarms; and gray-haired ladies in polyester pants the color of Barney checking out cookwear. But we also saw a good number of Aprica strollers and Versace tees. Just like the infomercial audience, fair-goers are predominantly middle-income families, with a sprinkling of high-end earners.

After a few of these trips, we realized there were three things you could count on: bad food, a Navy or Marine recruitment booth, and some guy pitching a slicer dicer.

His routine was always the same. He would have a big platter of ornately carved carrots, squash, cucumbers, onions, and tomatoes. Next to this bountiful display was a bowl of the same vegetables in their natural, presliced state. He'd reach for an onion.

"Ladies, I'll bet you've shed more tears over an onion than a husband." Giggles. "How often do you make coleslaw, ladies? Everybody likes coleslaw but nobody wants to make it." He'd choose his victim. "Does your husband get it once a month, lady?" More laughter. He'd roll his eyes. "Hey folks, I'm talking *coleslaw* here." If someone walked away, he'd bang on the table. "Where you goin'? I haven't asked for any money yet." No one else would dare to leave. He'd start all over again every 15 minutes. There was even a cardboard clock on the wall to indicate the next "showtime."

It occurred to me that holding people's attention at a fair was easier than holding it in their living room or bedroom. At home, where they felt secure and comfortable, if they grew bored or weren't interested they could change the channel or turn off the TV. I'd have to remember that.

A few products caught my eye on these trips. First, the Sasson iron. It was a high-pressure steam iron that allowed you to iron drapes without taking them down. The wrinkles came right out. Talk about an effective demonstration! I approached the woman selling it, but she said she was already talking to someone in the direct-response industry, someone "established." In other words, take a hike, pal. My instincts were good, though. The Sasson iron ultimately became a huge hit.

I also considered a food dehydrator. I saw it on a table, with lots of brochures around it. There were photographs of the food you could make on the wall. But the salesperson appeared bored. I looked at this thing and thought to myself, "How many people get up in the morning and say they gotta have beef jerky?" I thumbed through the brochure. It was a lot of work. You had to buy the beef, cut it up, salt it down, lay it on the trays, let it dry for three days. Wasn't it simpler to go down to 7-Eleven?

I just didn't get it. But Ron Popeil, Mr. Veg-O-Matic, did. He had a big hit with the Ronco Food Dehydrator. He sold a couple million through long-form infomercials and appearances on QVC Network, the home-shopping channel. Think of the money you'll save, and the fun you'll have, he told viewers, making your own banana chips, soup mix, and potpourri! He had a bunch of dehydrators going at once: one for dried fruit, one for fish jerky, one for turkey jerky. He laid out the finished products; everything looked delicious. You could lick the TV screen. Where Popeil saw beauty and abundance, I'd seen only an endless line of dried beef. Randee tried to console me later: "Think of all the studio heads who turned down *Star Wars*." Fortunately in my business, as in the movie business, you're remembered for the right decisions more than the wrong ones.

A staple of the pitch market are pots and pans. At the Long Beach Home Remodeling and Decorating Show in California, Pippa and I watched a demonstration for Pro HG Cooking Pans. They're high-grade alloy pans. Their selling point is that they're durable and you don't have to use cooking oil, which is better for your health. I had no intention of making pots and pans my first infomercial product, but my feet were tired so I agreed to sit down.

The salesman fried an egg in one of them without any oil and it didn't stick. Next, he took a hammer and whacked the pan. The audience gasped, but not a mark was made. He had a panoply of pans, every possible shape and size, for every possible purpose—saucepans, saute pans, double-boilers, frying pans, omelette pans. Most of the audience were elderly women. (Who else has the time to watch a cooking demonstration in the middle of the afternoon?)

He waxed eloquent about the virtues of lids with vents. He told jokes: "Any of you ladies like to bake? Do you happen to know where Betty Crocker is? She's in the hospital. Burned her buns."

Ha, ha, ha.

Now, he shifted gears. He unrolled a giant poster and held it high. "Which one of these pans do you want, ma'am?" he asked a blue-hair up front. She pointed to the picture. To my surprise, more than a few women purchased a pan.

He looked at Pippa.

"Ma'am, which one would you like to start with?" She eyed the poster. "I'll take them all." The guy's jaw dropped. I'm sure no one had ever bought an entire set from him, not at $2,000. "Make it two sets," she added, creating the very real possibility of cardiac arrest. Turning to me, she chirped, "I'll have one for the Vermont house." Right. The begonia farm.

Four thousand dollars' worth of pots and pans.

I'm trying to get a business off the ground and she's decorating her kitchen!

The rich *are* different.

CHAPTER · 3

An Irresistible Product

Leslie was on the phone with a convention and visitors bureau. She made it a habit to call at least a half-dozen cities every few weeks to inquire about home shows, garden shows, and county fairs. Thanks to her diligence I was on the road most of the time. Yet after three months all I had to show for it was a collection of tiny shampoo bottles and enough frequent flier miles for a trip to New Zealand. No product, no spokesperson, nothing.

The pressure was on.

Leslie scribbled something onto her legal pad. I peered over her shoulder. *Miami . . . home show . . . November.* Hmm. She hung up the phone. "You wanna go?" she said.

"Fine."

"Where would you like to stay?"

"The Fontainebleau," I replied, for no other reason than I'd heard of it. My knowledge of Miami was scant and rather dated. Jackie Gleason. Hialeah. The Fontainebleau.

Three weeks later, I was on the plane. By the time I touched down at the airport, I was feeling optimistic. I'd also had two Dewars on the rocks. *This trip will be successful,* I repeated to myself like a mantra. I rented a car and headed for the hotel. I was supposed to take the Airport Expressway to the Julia Tuttle Causeway, but I guess I missed a turn. I hadn't planned on it, but I saw a good deal of Little Havana.

I made a few corrections and crossed Biscayne Bay.

Driving north on Collins Avenue, it struck me that Miami Beach had more in common with Manhattan than Los Angeles. Like Manhattan, it's an island. But it's also urban. The hotels that line both sides of the street have all the charm of housing projects: lots of concrete and chipped cement. The traffic is vicious. And you can't see the beach. I don't know about you, but my idea of a great vacation is lying in a hammock on a remote island, a balmy breeze on my skin. I couldn't fathom how anyone could pay for *this.* Yet there were tour buses aplenty.

For someone trying to strike it rich in an industry perceived as lowbrow, the Fontainebleau was perfect. Kitschy in the extreme, it looks like Liberace designed it. He did not; Morris Lapidus holds that distinction. When it was completed in 1954, the Bauhaus crowd loathed it; the average Joe and his wife loved it. (Versailles meets ancient Rome meets Esther Williams!) So did Hollywood. The James Bond movie *Goldfinger* opens at The Fontainebleau. I was delighted with the place until I got to my room. I had a nice view of the water, but the windows were welded shut; it was like looking at the ocean on television. So much for balmy breezes and the lulling sound of the surf.

I'd had it with driving, so I grabbed a cab. I asked the driver if he knew of a good Cuban restaurant. Nothing fancy, I told him. He dropped me off at what appeared to be a diner. I ordered ceviche, crispy chicken with black beans, and plantains. *Heaven.*

From there I took a cab to South Beach. The South Beach Historic District is where you find all those renovated art deco hotels that have been hyped to death in recent years. From my sidewalk table where I had coffee and dessert, I watched the parade of fashionably dressed young people, gay couples, models, and chain-smoking photographers with Italian accents. It reminded me of Sunset Plaza, a chic stretch along Sunset Boulevard, the principal difference being that in South Beach the "beautiful people" talked about clothes and photo shoots, not the movie business.

Next morning I headed to the home show. I'd been to enough of these things to know better than to comb every aisle and to stop at every booth. Instead, I searched out the largest crowds. A big crowd means the product is captivating or that the pitchman is superb. Maybe both.

Laughter, gasps, howls. I followed my ears. As I drew closer, I heard a melodious patter. Two aisles over, there he was: a cocky, bouncy man talking at high speed as he sliced a knife through a package of frozen vegetables, "... and you never have to sharpen it!"

He picked up a hammer. "This is for the skeptics," he said, dropping it with a bang onto the cutting board. Sure enough, he began sawing into the metal head with a kitchen knife. He held up a piece of white paper covered with flecks of metal. "The shavings don't lie, folks, the shavings don't lie. You'll do ham bones, steak bones, chicken bones . . ."

Now he grabbed a tomato but kept right on talking.

"But the truest test of a knife is still a red, ripe tomato." Paper-thin slices fell from the blade. "Will ya look at that, folks."

Nothing was safe from harm. Fruits. Vegetables. Steak. "I'm tellin' ya, folks, fish will roll outta their skins," he said reaching for a filet knife.

He was deft; he was dramatic. He was funny. And the amazing thing was, he had these short, stubby fingers. Yet they just *danced*.

Then he did something curious. He laid the knife down on the table and clapped his hands, hard enough to hurt. (I asked him later what the clap was about. He explained that in the first part of his pitch he's gathering a crowd and building interest in the product. The clap breaks the spell of entertainment, signaling it's time to open your wallet.)

"Here's the deal, folks. This offer won't last long. Buy the first knife for nineteen ninety-five and I'll throw in a second one, *plus* the paring knife and filet knife, absolutely free." He couldn't collect the money fast enough. People were waving bills in the air.

The salesman's name was Tony Notaro. He was born in Brooklyn, six blocks from Coney Island, where he used to hang out as a kid. He'd been a pitchman on the fair circuit for years and was a protege of the legendary Arnold Morris ("king of the pitchmen"), who introduced *The Blade, The Great Wok of China,* and *The Daily Mixer,* three early infomercial hits for Quantum Marketing. (A bit of history: Morris is Ron Popeil's cousin. Both men started their careers as hucksters for their fathers' inventions and cut their teeth on the Atlantic City Boardwalk. A lot of people got their start as hucksters. Dick Clark, for example, and Ed McMahon, who quit managing his father's bingo hall when he realized how much money he could make pitching kitchen gadgets for Arnold Morris' brother!)

I watched Tony's show three times. After the third cycle, I said to myself, that's it, here's my man. All I need is a product. (I didn't want to do knives. I couldn't get excited about them.) Tony and I exchanged cards, and I rushed to catch my plane back to Los Angeles. All the way home, my mind was occupied with one thought: *What would Tony sell?* By this time, word had gotten out that there was a new infomercial company in town and we had received a lot of submissions.

I knew I needed something with mass appeal because television is a mass medium. (A product with narrow appeal, say, a hunting rifle, doesn't work on TV because the rates you pay for media are based on total viewership and only a small percentage of people are interested in hunting. Better to use a narrow-cast medium, a magazine like *Field & Stream.*) I also needed to stay clear of commodity products like nuts and bolts or garden hose. One brand is pretty much like another, so the buying decision is based on who's got the lowest price. There's not much margin in these products. I needed a value-added product, something that offered a distinct advantage, which would justify a higher price.

And, as I told Pippa, it had to withstand retail scrutiny. My whole strategy was to create brand loyalty, which could be exploited in retail. (TV products are attractive to discount merchandisers like Kmart and Target, which can provide broad, national distribution in a matter of months while your campaign is hot.)

With all this in mind, I worked through my list of potential products. Some were mainstream. Some were more wacky:

- *Sheffield's Gold Solution.* Here was a great product. I saw an ad in a catalogue for a liquid that coated ordinary metal with gold. You dipped your jewelry into this stuff and—presto—gold plating! Great demonstration and a vast market in home jewelry repair and with hobbyists. But the manufacturer's price was too high, which meant I couldn't turn a profit. There's a rule-of-thumb in the direct-response business that you need a 5-to-1 ratio between your retail price and your cost of buying or making the product. Half of your retail price goes to media costs, and the other half includes product, telemarketing (i.e., inbound telephone service), warehousing, shipping, and insurance. What's left over is profit.
- *Prolong.* An oil additive for your car engine. Good product, huge potential market in both direct response and retail. True, STP had been on the market for years—but what got me was a jaw-dropping demonstration. I traveled to a warehouse in Orange County, where I watched mechanics and engine experts perform a series of impressive lubrication stress tests. For a finale, they drained all the oil out of an engine. All that separated metal from metal was a thin coating of Prolong. Then they started the engine, revving it higher and higher. I have to tell you, I was sweating. But the engine didn't seize, didn't blow up. I was sold. Though I tried, I couldn't acquire the rights, and last

I heard they were still trying to bring the product to market. A similar product became a huge hit in 1992: Dura-Lube. The dramatic demonstration in the Dura-Lube infomercial was startlingly similar to the one I'd witnessed in that warehouse in Orange County.

- *Breakaway 2000.* A true novelty. It was a computerized cigarette case that helped you quit smoking. It released only a certain number of cigarettes a day. Neat product, but I couldn't figure out the right creative concept. Finally, I came to the conclusion that anti-smoking campaigns have an inherent marketing problem, which is, they ask you to dump your best friend. Not a good candidate for an impulse purchase.

- *Speedee-Gro* (or was it Speedee-Plant?) A set of cassette tapes for orchards and cornfields developed by a farmer. Fruit-bearing trees that listened to the music—I think it was altered Mozart—produced fruit in half the time as did trees left to grow in silence. Ditto for corn. The farmer had amazing documentation, including comparative photos and university studies. Maybe it was the fertilizer he included that did most of the work, but the music was a great marketing hook. My thought was to expand the market to city-dwellers. I pictured flower boxes overflowing with petunias and geraniums. But I couldn't make a deal with him.

Infomercials promote more than their share of kooky products. There's a reason: marketing people dominate the industry. They have neither the manufacturing background nor the financing to do product development. So they look for a product with an obvious sales angle and easily acquirable rights..

But if I make but one point clear in this book, it's this: Infomercials are not just about hair-in-a-can. Any manufacturer with an appealing mass-market product can use a national direct-response television campaign to build brand awareness to achieve accelerated national retail distribution.

Back to my product search.

Having scratched all of the above off the list, I was left with no list. Luckily, Tony knew a guy who was a good source for new product ideas. He gave me his phone number. I don't remember his name, but I remember he was Israeli. (I never met him. He remains a mysterious figure.) In a thick accent he told me about a chemical manufacturer outside Atlanta, Georgia. The company made a powder that, when added to water, turned the water into a solid. I got hold of some. It was magical stuff. I hadn't seen a demonstration as dramatic since Prolong. A tiny amount of powder turned a big puddle into a dry slush you could scoop up with your hands, vacuum away, or sweep up with a broom and dustpan. Originally created for industrial uses like spills in hospitals or on airport runways, the company had been trying to market it for home use.

I told Randee and her writing partner, Laurie, about it. What's wrong with paper towels? they said. What did they know; they wrote screenplays. I was confident millions of housewives would be crazy for the stuff.

Conventional wisdom maintained that you could only sell one product in an infomercial. I decided to ignore that rule. Like many newcomers to the business, I thought more could be better. The multiple offer also solved another problem for me: the most I could charge for Gone alone was $19.95, too low a price point to support a long-form infomercial. In retrospect, I should've been more open to short-form.

The company had two other products: a fabric spray that was like a super Scotchgard, and these handy stain-remover cloths you carried in your pocket or purse for on-the-spot cleaning. I decided to license all three products. I'd build the infomercial around the miracle powder, offer the fabric protector as part of the deal, and mention the stain remover at the end, just to goose 'em. A complete cleaning arsenal. We named the powder Gone, the fabric protector Shield, and the spot remover Stain Out.

I flew Tony in, put him up at the Sunset Hyatt, treated him like a star. Why not?—we wanted him to turn in a stellar performance. He and I got to work on the ad. We spent days pacing back and forth in Pippa's conference room, living on delivered pizzas and Cokes. We discussed the show's format. With products that demonstrate this spectacularly, a live demonstration show was an obvious choice; we called it *Seeing Is Believing.* The copy strategy, we decided, would be classic infomercial—*this stuff will solve your problems.* Quicker, easier, costs less money.

Tony had a black belt in karate. When he needed to relax, to blow off some steam, he pretended to kick me in the chin. For a chubby guy he wore awfully tight pants. I worried more for the pants than my chin.

At the end of each day, a young man named Bill Heichert stopped by the office. He worked for Tony; he pitched products at different venues around Los Angeles. He'd drop a huge pile of cash onto the conference table, and Tony would count the money and give him his cut. Bill had pitched everything—mops, slicers, synthetic chamois, knives, you name it. He could speak carney, too. I asked him once to drop a few words, but he refused. He seemed embarrassed, carnival barkers being rather low on the social scale. Today, he and a partner head up a handful of infomercial marketing and manufacturing companies in La Mirada, California, and Bill drives a Mercedes convertible.

Anyway, when Tony and I were happy with the script, I gave it to Pippa. She made a few suggestions but was pleased overall. I had decided to do a demonstration show, as that format would show up Tony's strength as a pitchman. He'd sprinkle Gone onto a carpet and vacuum up the mess with a flourish. He'd spray Shield onto a white couch and marvel at how the grape juice he'd thrown on it slid off without a trace. Magic.

Of course, magic can be improved upon.

Gaffing, or faking something for visual or dramatic effect, is a fine Hollywood tradition. Alan Ladd was short, so the gaffers dug a hole for his leading lady to stand in during his love scenes. If an actor arrives on the set with puffy eyes from boozing it up the night before, nothing takes care of it as quickly as a dab of Preparation H.

But an infomercial is different. It's about sales, not entertainment. The products you demonstrate have to work as well at home as they do on the show and *without* the help of gaffers. That's assuming you're an ethical producer. I knew I had a problem when the two studio propmen I'd hired proudly showed me the varnished shirt they'd created for the Stain Out demonstration. Can't use it, I said. Well, they countered, how about twelve coats of Shield on the couch before the cameras start rolling? Sorry, just one. You're the boss, they said, but we *will* use a spill-resistant carpet for the Gone demo, right?

Wrong! They just didn't get it.

The temptation to gaff a demonstration is hard to resist. The showman and the salesman in you push you to do it. Some people succumb. Several years ago, hand mixers were the rage. They lent themselves to amazing demonstrations—whipped potatoes in seconds, applesauce in an instant, and skim milk to "whipped cream" in no time at all. One of the mixer infomercials, it was reputed, used a hidden voltage regulator for a more dramatic demonstration of the product's effectiveness.

Direct response involves degrees of manipulation, but so does conventional advertising. I'll bet a lot of models in toothpaste ads owe their dazzling smiles more to their expensive caps than to their brushing habits. And cars in our hands never turn and stop as precisely as the ones driven by stunt drivers in the television ads. But there's a difference between showing your product in the best light and creating a false impression. Where does shrewd marketing end and deception begin? It's a question you face as an advertiser. About all I can say is, let your conscience be your guide.

Now, because I'd chosen to have a live audience, I needed to shoot in real time, the style perfected in TV sitcoms. Directing that kind of show is a specialized job; I couldn't do it myself. (Though I'd directed my how-to videos at Landsburg, I didn't dare attempt this.) So I hired a director with a lot of three-camera experience, specifically talk shows and game shows.

Directing three cameras—*live*—is a tricky business. The director sits in a production booth and watches the monitors, each tracking a different camera angle. A headset provides a link to the camera operators down on the set and to the stage manager, who relays the director's comments to the talent.

The night before the shoot, we walked through the script with the director, the stage manager, and the camera operators. The director showed Tony his *marks,* that is, where to stand at various points in the show. For the opening, he instructed him to look at camera one. When he walked to the demonstration area to pour Gone on the floor, camera two would be on him. Then it would be back to camera one. Camera three was for wide-angle shots. Tony looked utterly confused. "Just look for the little red light on top of the camera," said the director impatiently.

Tony was perspiring.

The next day was the shoot. It would be live-to-tape, which means we'd shoot it as though it were live but we'd have the option to stop if need be.

When I arrived at the studio I discovered these spectacular bouquets of flowers in the dressing rooms. They were from Pippa. The dressing rooms, mind you, were little more than holes in the wall.

She arrived early. She wanted to meet the director, the camera and prop people, *everyone.* She shared a laugh with the makeup artist. After flitting about for a half hour, she settled into one of the canvas director's chairs we had ringing the set. She was clearly enjoying this. She had more experience in front of a camera than anyone else there, and she knew it.

"Nervous?" she asked impishly.

"Not really," I lied. "But Tony is. He's not used to being on camera."

"Oh, he'll be fine. The butterflies will pass."

I wasn't so sure. While Pippa was charming the stage crew, I'd spent the last 30 minutes trying to build up Tony's confidence. This wasn't a demonstration booth at a fair or a home show. The audience wasn't *real*—just a bunch of bored people I'd paid to clap on cue. And then there were the 25 jaded film professionals. They wanted to be home in time for *Cheers.* Worse, they all knew each other. Tony was the outsider.

We did a run-through. "And now the star of our show, Tony Notaro!" boomed the announcer. Tony strode onto the set. "Let's talk about spills. . . ." he began. He remembered his lines—he didn't stumble—but you could tell he was concentrating too hard. He reached for the bottle of Gone, then lifted his head to look for the camera. Oops, wrong one. I winced.

From the kitchen table, he scurried over to the pyramid of paper towels, then to the couch, then circled back to the kitchen table, then hustled over to the mannequins wearing men's suits. He was on his knees; he was squatting. He was up, he was down. But it was an effort for him. It was like watching someone run an obstacle course. Someone out of shape.

And he wasn't funny. The audience barely tittered. And they were paid.

"See what I mean?" I said to Pippa.

She gave him a sidelong glance. Then she did something I'll never forget. She stood up and walked over to him and put her arms around him. "Dance with me, Tony. Dance with me," I heard her say. Tony blushed, but he was game. He rose to the occasion. They waltzed around the studio; around the cameramen and the lighting technicians, around the TelePrompTer operator, the key grip, and the floor manager. When they reached me, they stopped. "Think of the camera as your dance partner," said Pippa. "Just think of it as your dance partner." And she walked away.

She was right, of course. You've got to court the camera. Forget everyone else in the room. That's what acting is all about. It was a marvelous moment.

But it meant I'd screwed up.

My first mistake was not giving Tony enough rehearsal time for him to feel totally comfortable on the set. One day isn't enough, even for TV guys like Ian Long and Mike Levey. My second mistake was hiring a director who was used to working with television professionals, people who can find the right camera and hit their marks in their sleep. I compounded the problem by ceding control to him. I should have told him to follow Tony's lead, to keep a camera on him and just let him do his thing. So what if everybody was out of focus? This wasn't a Merchant-Ivory production. It was an infomercial.

71

At the end of twelve agonizing hours came the coup de grace. I overheard a cameraman say to the stage manager during yet another take of Tony sprinkling Gone on a spill, "I dunno. Wouldn't it be easier to use a paper towel?"

Ouch.

The ad aired on a Friday in six cities. If the phones rang like crazy—and I prayed that they would—we'd buy more media time.

It was a long, *long* weekend. I called the telemarketing company every hour to see how many orders we'd received. I made the calls from my house, from my basement office. I'd place the call, learn that the phones were silent, then slowly trudge upstairs to tell Randee. As the hours passed, it became harder and harder to reach for the phone. By Sunday, I didn't have to. It was clear we'd bombed.

I'd made several bad choices. The most fundamental was I'd chosen the wrong product. Great demonstration, but who needed it? I compounded the problem by trying to sell three products in one show and by not scheduling enough rehearsal time for my star, who later set sales records on QVC with his Kitchen Wizard slicer.

I didn't sleep well that night. But by Monday afternoon, I'd made two important resolutions: I'd consider short-form for the next show, and, more importantly, when choosing the next product, I wouldn't let myself be seduced by a splashy demonstration.

Pippa, bless her heart, took it in stride. She was in the game for seven more shows. If the first one didn't fly, perhaps the second one would: That's what I'd said in the business plan. Right then, she had more confidence in me than I did.

There are a lot of reasons an infomercial can fail. The first among them is choosing the wrong product. I made that mistake but so have others, and it's instructive to look at a few examples:

- *Bonfit patterner.* An example of a good-looking show, produced by a top-notch production company, hosted by an excellent spokesperson, Susan Ruttan, from *L.A. Law*—and a flop. The product was a plastic drafting and design system that promised to "revolutionize the art of home sewing." I believe the show failed because the product appeared too complicated. The subliminal message was that you needed a Ph.D. in engineering to use it.

- *Lean Solutions.* There are a lot of failures in the diet-show category, and this was one of them. It featured as the hosts, Robert Wagner, who I still consider to be a fine spokesperson, and Jill St. John. Joe Weider pitched the product. The problem, as I see it, was that there were too many food supplements on the market already and many of them were quite a bit cheaper. If you are going to enter a crowded field, you need to show compelling product advantages to survive.

- *Elimin-8.* A stain remover show that came too soon after the wildly successful SRX-11, which followed Stainarator, an earlier show, which followed the mega-hit Didi-Seven. Timing is everything in this business. Although certain product categories are perennials (who'd have thought after Ginsu 2000, there'd be room for the Miracle Blade?), an adequate amount of time must pass before the next clone hits the air.

And then there are the shows that have failure written all over them, but their success defies explanation. The legendary example? Flowbee.

There is no rhyme or reason why the Flowbee Home Haircutting System is such a monster hit. It's a haircutting contraption that attaches to your vacuum cleaner. (No, I'm not kidding.) The cheesy ad features satisfied Flowbee customers gushing about saving time and money as their hair gets sucked up into the thing. It's like a *Saturday Night Live* skit—or an Ed Wood movie. But inventor Rick Hunts had the last laugh: For several years in a row it's been one of the top 30 infomercials in the country, with more than $25 million in sales.

The Flowbee reminds us all that we're never as smart as we think we are.

After the Gone fiasco I decided to approach choosing a product more logically. I'd blown a lot of money and had nothing to show for it. Then, as now, there were six dominant infomercial product categories, and I weighed each of them carefully:

73

- *Beauty/Personal Care/Diet.* Dominated by a few monster hits over the last few years. Susan Powter. Victoria Principal. Sarah Purcell. Richard Simmons. But lots of celebrity flops, too: infomercial failures from Dolly Parton, Linda Evans, Raquel Welch. Expensive to produce, rarely less than $250,000 a pop. The show has to look beautiful if it hopes to sell a product to make *you* look beautiful. You need more lights to create the highlights and eliminate shadows in close-ups, you need more takes because there are more angles to shoot, and you need more time for hair and make-up. It all adds up.
- *Health and Fitness.* A perennial category. From Bruce and Kris Jenners' Power Trainer ($28 million in sales) to Covert Bailey's Health Rider (over $200 million in sales), the phones keep ringing. This category had more hit shows in the top 30 in 1995 than any other infomercial category, according to Jordan Whitney's *Green Sheet,* the industry newsletter that reviews and tracks new infomercials.
- *Business Opportunities.* A difficult category. Though real-estate investment shows launched the infomercial industry, there are few recent examples of success. An exception is Don LaPre's *Money-Making Secrets,* about buying and selling, auctions, and getting into the 900 number business. This category includes a spate of shows about starting home businesses. They failed because of poor copy strategy: They emphasized the features of working at home (no commute, no suits) but neglected to communicate the compelling promise: "You'll make more money!"
- *Self-Improvement.* Lots of winners here, including Tony Robbins' *Personal Power,* Kathy Lee Gifford and Frank Gifford's show about marriage and relationships, and the show featuring Barbara De Angelis, the former radio shrink from L.A. (Yes, I'd heard her on the radio. Yes, I'd approached her about doing a show. But I had to drop the ball when ThighMaster came along. Wish I'd had the time to pursue her.)
- *Automotive/Housewares.* From the Smart Mop to Ron Popeil's Food Dehydrator to the Contour Pillow to Power Foam, the

most fertile category. An endless stream of inventions and innovations. The shows are comparatively cheap to produce, as little as $20,000: The demonstration is the show, so you don't need a celebrity; the products lend themselves to short-form, and you can shoot in less than a day. Big retail and foreign potential.

- *Entertainment/Hobbies/Sports.* This category is dominated by Time-Life books and videos about the supernatural, gardening, wars, and more. Other recent successes include the Helicopter Lure (a fishing lure), Barbie as Scarlett, and Medicus Pro, a golf training device. I considered a Nat King Cole collection of CDs. I wanted to buy the rights to a PBS documentary about him to use in the infomercial, but they were too expensive.

Having analyzed these product categories, I decided to focus on only two: health and fitness, and automotive and housewares. Why? Because they lent themselves to short-form and were cheap to produce. Quite frankly, I was worried about running through Pippa's money so quickly.

Serendipity struck again. I received a phone call from my accountant.

A phone call from my accountant, mind you, was as welcome as hives. But to my surprise he had something interesting to say. And he got to the point quickly. He said he had a client, Josh Reynolds, who was marketing some kind of exercise equipment (great!) and was looking for additional financing. Would I like to meet with him?

Tell me more, I said, and he obliged.

Reynolds was an entrepreneur from Laguna Beach with a background in product development and marketing. He'd been responsible for perhaps the biggest fad ever to hit the jewelry industry, the mood ring. In 1975 he introduced what he called the Mood Stone, a liquid crystal that responded to heat by changing color. The medical industry used liquid crystal to detect the presence of cancerous tumors and determine stress levels by applying it to the skin. He simply applied it to jewelry. (So did others.

Rarely is a concept in the jewelry industry unique enough to be patentable.) His Mood Stone came with a pamphlet explaining how to relax and curb stress using a simple biofeedback technique.

Josh was a believer. He had studied biofeedback at the Menninger Clinic in Topeka, Kansas, and yoga with gurus from India. Then he established his own biofeedback clinic. A job on Wall Street drove him to it: When he was 28 and pulling down $250,000 a year working for takeover tycoon Asher Edelman, he got burned out and quit. He had appeared on *The Merv Griffin Show* to demonstrate the power of biofeedback techniques. (He claimed he could stop his heart for five seconds. He told me later he had to prove he could do it to get onto the show. Alas, when the time came to do it in front of an audience, he couldn't. Too nervous.) His business partner was Les Sinclair, who'd quit his job as a producer on *Griffin* to team up with Josh.

I had nothing to lose. I told my accountant to have Reynolds call me to set up a meeting.

When Josh arrived at my office he was wearing jeans and tennis shoes and carrying a large box under his arm. We walked into the conference room, where he placed the box on the table. He opened it up and pulled out a curious object.

"This is the V-Toner," he said.

From what I could tell, it was two wire loops covered with foam with a spring in the middle. He promptly started demonstrating all its uses. He worked on his biceps, his triceps, his abs and his pecs. (Now I knew why he showed up in jeans and sneakers.) When he finished, he handed it to me.

"We're pitching it as a gym-in-a-bag," he said.

It felt solid. "Good product."

"Yes it is. Made in America."

"Did you invent this?" I asked him.

"No. A Swedish chiropractic doctor invented it years ago to help skiers with fractures stay fit while stuck in bed. They used it to exercise their good leg, so it wouldn't wither."

"He's in Sweden?"

"She. No. She runs The Ashram."

Living in L.A., I knew all about The Ashram, the fabled boot-camp-style health spa where celebrities pay a couple of grand a week to hike miles under the blazing sun and dine on sprouts and broccoli for dinner.

"When I met her," Josh continued, "she was calling it the V-Bar. I changed the name. She'd sold a few of 'em, well, more than a few, but mostly to people she knew. It had a V shape, but there were no loops, and it was heavy-looking. I mean, it was all metal, except for two round pads on the end. It wasn't a pretty design. I showed it to friends of mine and they said it looked like something doctors might use to spread people's legs apart. Or an instrument of torture. It scared them. It was also too expensive to produce."

Josh said he spent three months trying to come up with a design that caught people's attention, if not consciously, then subconsciously.

I handed it back to him.

"If you hold it up like this," he said, lifting it in the air, "it looks like butterfly wings. And that's what came to me in a half-dream at two o'clock in the morning when my wife was beside me. Butterfly wings. The infinity symbol. All of a sudden, it was like everything came together, you know what I mean?"

Wow.

"Not only is the design attractive," he continued, "but it works. The wings, I mean, the loops, make good handles. You can tuck it under your arm and into the curve of your stomach. You can put it between your knees and work on your thighs, like this." He started squeezing.

"What's it cost to manufacture?"

"About five bucks," he said, as he worked on his quads.

I did a quick unit cost analysis in my head. Five bucks for the product, two dollars for packing and warehousing, three dollars to get the phone answered, another two dollars in miscellaneous costs like credit card charges and insurance, and three dollars to cover profit, overhead, and royalties. If I could sell it for $29.95, that left $15 to cover the media, and that seemed reasonable. Of course, I had absolutely no idea *how* to sell the thing. "Your're targeting women, right? I mean, the foam handles are a deep blue." (It's commonly accepted in marketing that women are attracted to blue.)

"Yes. Although we could add an element of red for men."

I turned the thing around in my hands. It was intriguing.

"Would you like to meet the inventor?" asked Josh, sensing interest.

"Yes, I think I would. What's her name?"

"Anne-Marie Bennstrom. You'll have to meet her at The Ashram."

The Ashram is hidden in a canyon of the magnificent Santa Monica Mountains, about twenty miles east of Malibu. I gave myself an hour to get there. It was an easy trip, mostly freeways, until I was five minutes away. Then it became maddening; I kept passing driveways to gated communities but couldn't find the road up into the canyon. To my left and right were white houses with red tile roofs with a lot of sun-baked ground in between. I pulled into one of the gatehouses to ask for directions. There was constant traffic in and out: maids in white uniforms, catering trucks, plumbers. No, the guard said, he had never heard of The Ashram. He pulled out a map and looked at it. "It's not on here," he said apologetically. I grabbed the map. He was right—it wasn't there. I thanked him and got back on the highway but reversed my direction.

Then I saw the road. I swear it hadn't been there before.

It quickly turned to dirt, my tires kicking up a cloud of dust behind me. As I climbed higher and higher, it occurred to me I might meet another car on its way down the mountain. What then? Suddenly I saw the tiniest of signs, shrouded in the bush. It was shaped like an arrow: THE ASHRAM, it said, pointing left. The road narrowed further and became more steep. Now I was really nervous. I maneuvered around a tight curve and boom, there it was: a suburban tract house. *This* was the famous Ashram? I laughed out loud.

As I got out of the car, I heard wind chimes. A woman who was rail-thin came out to greet me. She was wearing a white Patagonia tennis shirt and red stretch pants cut below the knee. She was barefoot. Her white-blonde hair was cut short; her eyes were grey and piercing. She appeared to be in her sixties. When she spoke she sounded like Garbo and had Garbo's androgynous quality.

She had a dog with her, a German shepherd she called Chakra. I followed her and the dog into the house and up the stairs to her office. A maid brought us some freshly squeezed orange juice.

"We have lots of time," she said. "The group is out on a fifteen-mile hike. They won't be back until 2 P.M." I wondered what movie stars or television executives were on the mountainside, panting under the sun. Maybe I'd meet Oprah Winfrey.

I asked her about her background. She stretched a bare foot up on her chair. As she spoke, she gazed out the window.

She'd built the five-bedroom house in 1974. The V-Bar had financed The Ashram. (She'd sold more than a few indeed.) She was the widow of Robert Prescott, the founder of Flying Tiger Airlines. She had managed the Golden Door spa in Escondido. Her best friend was Shirley MacLaine.

It got even more interesting.

When she was 24 years old, she drove her old Ford as far south as the Guatemalan border, where she got out of the car and walked into the jungle. All she had was a machete, a block of brown sugar, a toothbrush, and a little bit of money. One day a boa constrictor mistook her for a tree trunk and slid down her shoulder and over her leg.

"It was an eternity, I tell you. But when it had slithered away, I missed it. It was my only contact for six months with any living thing."

She shifted in her chair. "So, baby, you want to make millions, eh?"

She caught me by surprise. I was still thinking about the snake.

"Well, I think with the right marketing, the V-Bar, I mean, the V-Toner, could sell. I think it has potential as a direct-response product," I stammered.

"Have you seen the commercials we made?"

"No, but I understand you did not have great success with them." I was being kind. Josh had shown me the numbers. They were dismal. Still, I liked the product.

"Well, the journey is the goal, baby."

"Yes," I agreed, confused.

"It is an elegant piece of equipment, no?"

"Oh, yes," I nodded. "I think women would like it. Women always want to lose a few pounds, right?"

"You know, I don't even weigh people when they come here. I don't see a difference between the body and the mind and the emotions. To me, the body is crystallized emotions. A body that is out of balance is emotions out of balance. A body that is fat, that is holding emotions in, is depriving its emotions of expression. . . ."

The telephone rang.

"Are you in good shape?" she asked the caller. "We'll make you lean, mean, hard, and hungry. *Very* hungry. Everyone needs to suffer so they can love themselves a little more," she said, smiling. I pointed to my watch, indicating that I had to get going. I could have stayed longer, but I was afraid she might offer me sprouts and broccoli for lunch.

"I'll be in touch," I whispered and waved good-bye.

When I got back to the office, I found Leslie and Joe taking turns squeezing the V-Toner. They said they couldn't help themselves. Over the next few days, I noticed when people came into the office—messengers, lunch appointments for Pippa—the same thing happened: Nobody could leave it alone.

It was irresistible.

A few days later, the video copies of Josh's commercials arrived at the office. I was eager to watch them. I wanted to see where

Josh had gone wrong. I sat back on the white couch with the white pillows and clicked on the VCR. I expected something awful.

But, you know, the spots weren't bad. On the contrary, they were well-directed and well-cast. Josh had done what he said, presented the product as a gym-in-a-bag. Handy. Convenient. The pacing was fine. The music was right. I was mystified. Why were the numbers so lousy? Why had the spots tested so poorly?

What, in short, was the problem?

I clicked off the television. This was going to be harder than I thought.

CHAPTER · 4

Shooting
Suzanne

I was changing Holly's diaper. It wasn't easy. She kept trying to turn over. I grabbed her Ernie doll and made him dance. Distracted, she squealed with delight.

"She looks a little red, sweetie," said Randee, handing me the Balmex, then picking up the conversation where we'd left it. We'd been talking about spokespeople. "You know," she said, "the person you ought to get is Jane Fonda."

I struggled to hold Holly's diaper in place while I slipped her diaper wrap over it. Yes, we used cloth diapers. Most of our friends with kids thought we were crazy.

"I don't think I could get her. She's made a ton of money off her videos."

But Randee was on the right track.

Thirty years ago women wore girdles, not jogging bras. Feminine beauty had little to do with fitness. Marilyn Monroe, Rosalind Russell, Jayne Mansfield; they looked soft and fleshy, like "Jell-O on springs," as Jack Lemmon put it in *Some Like It Hot*. With help from Jane Fonda, whose exercise videos dominated the home-video market, the aerobics craze of the '80s defined a new look—a slender, decidedly athletic figure. But there was also the women's movement to thank. Today, Helen Reddy would sing: "I am strong, I am invincible . . . I am woman with 'Buns of Steel.' "

While Randee got Holly dressed, I headed into the living room to consider the V-Toner. We had it on the coffee table, like a knicknack. I started thinking about Josh's commercials. Maybe he had promised too much. Maybe I should focus on a single part of the body. But what part did women most want to improve? And what need was not being addressed by another product?

I picked up the V-Toner and started working my tricep muscles. *Are women concerned about dangling underarms?* Yeah, but not enough to go running to the phone.

I swung my feet onto the couch and did a few stomach crunches. Hmph. Offers good resistance. But it's too strenuous. Besides, it's too soon after the Abdomenizer by Fitness Quest.

I sat up straight, working my pecs. *Did women want to strengthen and tone their chests?* Probably. But a bust developer seemed so dated.

I put the V-Toner between my legs and started squeezing.

I knew a lot of women were dissatisfied with their thighs and spent hours in the gym looking for illusory perfection.

I felt my thigh muscles tightening. A good sign.

Squeeze, squeeze. Hmm. Feels comfortable. A pleasing exercise. You can do it while watching TV!

Randee appeared with Holly in her arms. "That's obscene!" she exclaimed and covered the baby's eyes with her hand. She was kidding, of course.

"Ya know, this is a great thigh exerciser," I said.

"Thighs?" she said. "Do you think women worry much about their thighs?"

My response, for which my wife is eternally grateful, was to totally ignore her. I knew I was on to something, even if it looked outrageous. Maybe people would laugh. Maybe it wouldn't work on TV. But if it did. . . .

Thighs. Shapely hips and thighs. This would be the promise that would sell the V-Toner. I'd deal with the titillation problem later.

First, I needed a spokesperson, a woman in her forties. I figured that would be the biggest market. Second, I wanted a celebrity.

Stars lend credibility to a show. When you're asking people to buy something they can't hold or touch, a recognizable face engenders trust. A celebrity also stops channel surfing. While clicking through the channels with the remote, searching for something worth watching, they land on your infomercial.

There's also the charisma factor. Celebrities have a special relationship with their public. They share a history. This is why Honda hires Jack Lemmon for a voice-over, for example. A familiar voice, like a familiar face, puts people at ease. In the case of an infomercial, where you're asking someone to buy a product, a celebrity's presence is disarming.

Sitting at my desk in the office, I scanned the list of talent I was considering. Every once in a while I'd shout out a name to get a reaction from Leslie and Hillary, Pippa's personal secretary.

"Whaddya think of Cathy Rigby?"

She had a lot to recommend her—an Olympic medal-winner in gymnastics, plus some acting credits, principally the musical *Peter Pan,* but Leslie and Hillary felt her appearance in a television commercial for a feminine hygiene product was a strike against her. (Although she's since done very well with her Fast Track exerciser.)

"Linda Gray?" They had to think a moment. Oh yeah, *Dallas.* Leslie gave her a thumb's up, Hillary, a thumb's down.

Suzanne Somers was also on the list. At first I dismissed her. At the time she was clearly yesterday's news. *Three's Company* was in the distant past, and her only TV show since then was a turkey called *She's the Sheriff,* mercifully seen by very few people. Then I started thinking: Maybe her fast fade was an advantage. When people saw her again, pitching my product and still looking knock-out gorgeous after all these years, maybe they'd think my product had something to do with it.

I started to look at Suzanne Somers more closely.

Like a lot of men, I remembered her bit part as the blonde in the T-bird in the 1973 film *American Graffiti.* By 1977 she was the toast of prime-time television opposite John Ritter and Joyce DeWitt as the adorable but vacuous Chrissy Snow. Then she blew it. In 1980, she asked for an increase in salary plus a percentage of the profits. The producers refused, and her character was written out of the show. *Three's Company* ran for another four years.

Down but not out, she dusted off her singing and dancing skills and performed in Las Vegas. Most impressive, with the help of her manager-husband Alan Hamel, she reinvented herself as a spokesperson for the children of alcoholics. (Her father was an alcoholic.) First came the 1988 bestseller *Keeping Secrets,* which chronicles her tortured childhood; then the Suzanne Somers Institute for the Effects of Addictions on the Family in Palm Springs, which spawned a chain of recovery centers; then a made-for-TV movie based on *Keeping Secrets;* then another book, *Wednesday's Children,* a collection of interviews with celebrities who'd survived abusive families . . . but, again, I'm getting ahead of myself.

At the time I circled her name with a red pen, she was on the rebound from *She's the Sheriff,* the show she'd hoped would be her comeback vehicle. When she wasn't in Vegas, she was traveling the country giving lectures to adult children of alcoholics. While personally gratifying, I'm sure, being a spokesperson for alcohol treatment centers was not what she had in mind when she threw away *Three's Company* with both hands. Her career badly needed jump-starting. This being the case, I thought I might get her.

Another reason Suzanne was at the top of my list was that she led her private life through a loudspeaker. She'd been tabloid fodder for years. This was *good.* It's not enough to hire a star—you want someone whose private life is common knowledge. That way, the audience feels like someone they know is talking to them.

Cher comes to mind. Farrah Fawcett comes to mind. Conversely, Mary Fran, who co-starred on *The Bob Newhart Show,* did three infomercials in 1994, and they all bombed. Why? In part because the public knew next to nothing about her. They were more familiar with the television character than the real person.

Somers and an exercise product were a good match. She was in great physical shape, plus she was warm and friendly; she wouldn't be intimidating. But a friendly and famous face is not enough. Dolly Parton's foray into infomercials was a disaster because she was clearly the wrong spokesperson for the product, which was makeup. Stage makeup, you might believe, but this was Dolly Parton's Confidence Makeup—"light as a feather" and "natural," as she said in the ad. (This from the woman who'd quipped, "It costs a lot of money to look this cheap.") Her fans love her, but I doubt they want to look like her. Meanwhile, a young Hollywood makeup artist, Victoria Jackson, has built a $300 million company based on sales from her infomercials. She's the right spokesperson for the product. But she made sure she had a celebrity guest, Meredith Baxter Birney, to spice up the show.

So using a celebrity doesn't guarantee success. You can have the right star and the right product and *still* go wrong. For instance, *Dynasty*'s Linda Evans found the right product—a skin-care system—but the infomercial failed because there was too much emphasis on the inventor's background as a cosmetic surgeon, which undercut the message about Primage skin cream. *Coach*'s Craig T. Nelson also found the right product, an engine oil additive called Slick 50. (He's an amateur racecar driver.) The show failed because Slick 50 was widely available in stores before the infomercial was launched, not because of the star.

According to Jordan Whitney's *Green Sheet,* only 17 out of the top 50 infomercials in 1994 featured celebrities. But would *Psychic Friends* have been such a monster hit without Dionne Warwick? I don't think so. Would American Telecast have sold $130 million worth of treadmills without Jane Fonda? Doubtful. Would the *Principal Secret* have ruled skin care for four years if the spokesperson had been Victoria from Peoria instead of Victoria Principal? Unlikely.

Another thing: It's crucial that stars project enthusiasm for the product, that they don't come off like they're doing it just for the money. (Which they are, of course—*big* money. Obviously the audience knows this, but you don't want them thinking about it.) They must "pitch from the heart." To their credit, Dolly Parton and Linda Evans oozed sincerity. Some celebs don't. I can't name names, but there was the star who, having been hired for an infomercial, refused to be shown touching the product. Can you believe it?

The point of this little diatribe is that some actors can't get past the embarrassment of standing up there and selling a product like a huckster. *And the embarrassment shows.* Acting the part of a spokesperson isn't that difficult; after all, it's not Shakespeare. What *is* difficult is ignoring the voices in your head screaming, "I shouldn't be here like a door-to-door salesperson. I'm an actress. I should be playing Ophelia." If celebrities believe they are above selling a product, a flat delivery or tight facial muscles or stiff body language will betray them; they will communicate *I don't want to be here.* Most actors feel that starring in *any* commercial— infomercial or not—is prostituting their gift. This is why big-name actors like Sylvester Stallone and Kevin Costner appear in commercials that run in Japan but not the United States: They want the money but they don't want to be associated with, God forbid, *selling.* Never mind that marketing overtook art in Hollywood *years* ago—why else is Stallone a star?

Lots of stars appear in infomercials, and it doesn't hurt them a bit—Jane Fonda, Cher, Kathie Lee Gifford, John Tesh, and Connie Selleca, for example. They've reaped the benefits. So have stars whose careers have stalled, such as Victoria Principal, Dionne Warwick, and Morgan Fairchild. In some cases, careers have expanded due to infomercials. Take Bruce Jenner and, more recently, Peggy Fleming, who turned her fading celebrity into a major revenue source. And for those whose careers seemed over, infomercials have provided retirement income. Just ask Dick Cavett who had a big hit with Harry Lorayne's Memory Course.

I called Suzanne's husband. I had his number because we'd had some discussions about shooting an exercise video based on her

Vegas routine. He said I should send them the product, so I did. A few weeks later he invited me to their home in Palm Springs. They wanted to talk.

Palm Springs. I've never liked it much. Because of the surrounding hills, the planes have to make this vertical drop onto the runway. And there's the baking heat.

A taxi dropped me off on a dirt road at the bottom of a hill. Like many houses in Palm Springs, Suzanne's and Alan's house is built into the side of what appears to be a moraine; it's a hike to the front door, so I was out of breath when Alan greeted me. We shook hands and sat down. There was some Latino music playing in the background.

"Nice music," I said, making conversation.

"*We* like it. You don't have to hear the words," said Alan.

Suzanne walked in. She looked prettier in person than on television. She was dressed casually, in jeans and a big, white shirt. Her hair looked sensational. She shook my hand and said she had to make some calls. She'd leave us guys to talk. But she wanted me to know that she'd used the product every day since she received it and that she could feel the difference, she said, running her hands down her hips. "I've got it next to my bed," she said, giggling.

With that, she disappeared. A moment later the music stopped.

"Let's talk outside, on the deck," said Alan and gestured for me to follow him.

It was sparsely furnished. No cushioned lounge chairs, no umbrella tables. Just benches. Wrought-iron benches. The spartan character of the deck was in keeping with the stark landscape: The hills looked nude. I sat down, or rather perched, on a bench, choosing the one closest to the wall of the house. I eyed the sun suspiciously.

Alan talked at length about the Institute, how they were setting up franchises around the country. I listened. He talked about growing up in Toronto. We discovered we'd both lived on Spadina Avenue, he as a child; me, for a summer during college. He asked if I'd ever gone to Shopsy's Deli. Of course, I said, it was one of my favorite places to eat in Toronto.

I'd taken the time to read Suzanne's book, so I already knew a great deal about him. His parents were Polish immigrants. Growing up, he endured a lot of antisemitism. He was beat up by the kids in his neighborhood on a daily basis. Before he was 14, he held a variety of jobs. He knew how to hustle for work. His deep voice got him a job in radio, and later, in television. He was famous in Canada and known to a degree in the States. He met Suzanne in Los Angeles when he was the host of a television show called *The Anniversary Game* and she was the model who posed next to the prizes—refrigerators and the like. Though no Robert Redford, he projected confidence. And why not? He was successful, glib, well-traveled. Still, I had this feeling he couldn't believe his good fortune, especially where Suzanne was concerned. He reminded me of Richard Dreyfuss's character in *American Graffiti,* only Alan *got* the blonde.

He stood up to stretch his legs, then motioned for me to follow him up the stairs to the next level. The deck was built in tiers, you see, like a wedding cake. I was glad for the chance to stand. My butt was killing me.

The minute we sat down again, I turned the conversation back to the product. I started to lay out my plans, and he interrupted to tell me that Suzanne had been doing all the exercises but the thigh exercises were her favorite.

Great. This was going to be easy. I threw out the name Thigh-Master, and his eyes lit up. They had thought of the name, too, he said. And we agreed on it right there.

"Let's talk about the design," he said. "Is this what it's going to look like?" From his tone, I couldn't tell if he thought it looked fine or if he thought it looked like crap.

"Well, the designer—his name is Josh Reynolds—is still working on it. He started with fuchsia handles but they skew too upscale. So, he chose blue—women like blue—and he wants to change the color of the plastic cap over the spring to lipstick red. He says the research shows that women prefer a lighter red. Men prefer dark red, like the color of dried blood. Goes back millions of years. Women gathered bright, red berries; men brought home dead animals. We're hard-wired, I guess."

He winked. "I have some knowledge of what women prefer."

"Let's talk dollars and cents," he said, standing up again. Now we moved to the third—and highest—level of the deck. Damn it. Same benches. I was parched by now, but I managed to speak.

I made him an offer.

"I don't wanna typical deal. I want a *net* deal," he said flatly. "If this thing flies, I want to benefit from it. I'm not looking for anything up front. I'm looking for significant participation."

This was good news. A net deal was better than a conventional deal. Typically, the star gets $10,000 to $200,000 in advance. The advance buys you the shoot, which usually lasts two to three days; one or two days of pick-up shots and voice-overs if you need them; and the right to test-market the ad for ninety days *outside* New York, Chicago, and Los Angeles. (This is important to stars. If the ad tests poorly, they don't want ad agencies to know because it will hurt them in future negotiations for other spokesperson jobs.)

During the ninety days, you buy limited media and test the show and decide if you'll roll out the program based on good test results or drop it. But before you roll out, you owe the star another advance, which can be very small or, in some exceptional cases, in the $1 million stratosphere. This payment and the first payment are called "advances," because they're advance payments against a gross royalty in the 3% to 5% range. When a show hits, this is where the big money is. Although it was widely reported that Dolly Parton was paid $2 million to star in her Confidence makeup show, the most offered a star for an infomercial, I'll bet she saw only $200,000 (my estimate of her first advance) since the infomercial was never rolled out.

But a net deal—what Alan proposed—usually doesn't call for an advance, and it was what I'd been praying for. I was worried about having enough money for the next shoot if this one failed. If I didn't have to pay a nickel up front for the talent, all the better.

It was twilight. "You boys doing okay?" asked Suzanne as she climbed up the steps of the deck.

"We're all through," said Alan, standing up. "You wanna show Peter to his car?" Geez, no invitation to dinner. They hadn't offered me a thing all afternoon. Not even water.

"Shall I take him in the funicular?"

"Yes, why don't you. It's too dark to take the stairs."

There was something in the way she asked the question and the way he answered her that suggested they were up to something.

We walked outside. The outline of the brown hills against the slate-blue, crepuscular sky was awesome. The hills looked like cardboard cutouts glued onto a swatch of velvet, like some child's art project. I could see lights twinkling in the distance.

Suzanne and I squeezed into the funicular. She pressed a button and we glided down the hill, on a track. There was barely room for two people. All of a sudden, her warm breath was on my cheek. "Peter," she whispered in my ear, "I just want you to know how excited I am about this project. I had the exact same feeling when I got the part on *Three's Company.* I'm telling you, this is going to be *big.* I'm going to make you *so* much money."

She opened the door of the funicular, air-kissed me good-bye, and sailed up the side of the hill in the moonlight. I chuckled. She was clearly heading off "buyer's remorse." It's an old celebrity trick. I think they learn it in star school. It was a good sign. It meant I had her.

Now I needed to write the script. I got into the waiting cab and headed to the airport.

The plane was one of those commuter prop jets. I was the sole passenger. Nevertheless, the pilot dutifully delivered the flotation cushion/oxygen mask/safety belt spiel, word for word. When he thanked "everyone" for choosing the airline, it was all I could do to stifle my laughter. When he finished, he returned to the cockpit, closed the door, and started the engines.

The take-off was wild. The climb was so steep, I felt like I was in a rocket. But that was nothing compared to what happened next. The plane shook violently, slamming down hard like it was hitting a surface thousands of feet up in the air. There was lightning flashing everywhere. We'd run smack into a thunderstorm.

Then the lights went out.

Not a peep from the cockpit.

I'm sitting in the dark, on a plane, lightning cracking all around me—alone. Any minute I expect to hear Rod Serling's voice:

Submitted for your approval. A businessman returning home from a successful meeting. He believes he has a deal in his pocket. That his wife and child are waiting. That someone's flying the plane. But things aren't always as they seem or as they should be. As our businessman will soon discover, the bizarre has many faces. Ladies and gentlemen, he has entered The Twilight Zone. . . .

When we landed I headed straight for the bar.

I called Jim McNamara, the copywriter I'd met when Tony Hoffman was shooting *Everybody's Money Matters* at Landsburg. I told him I needed some help with the copy strategy. He said he was busy, up to his ears in work, but he'd do what he could. (He did more than that. He wrote most of the script—and it's a classic.)

A few days later he came into the office. I showed him the V-Toner, which I now referred to as the ThighMaster. Jim squeezed it with his arms a few times, sat down, and put it between his thighs.

"Kind of sexy, isn't it?" he grinned.

"Titillating," I rejoined.

"Well, let's use it to our advantage," he said brightly, while working his thigh muscles.

I told him I'd already worked out what I called the "meaningful promise": "Squeeze, *squeeze* your way to shapely hips and thighs." The secondary promise was, yes, it gives you a good upper body workout, too. But the main selling point was that it would benefit the hips and thighs.

A few days later, Jim called in a headline. A good headline is catchy. "Okay, Peter. Here it is: 'You may not have been born with great legs, but now you can look like you were.' " I liked it. Jim had struck the right tone. First, it implied that Suzanne Somers, who you hadn't seen in *years,* looked sensational because she'd

95

been using ThighMaster. It also made her seem less threatening. She, a glamorous TV star, had to work at looking good, just like the television viewer did. But I insisted we change the "you" to "we."

Following Jim's lead, I wrote an inclusionary statement that supported the headline: "I used to do aerobics till I dropped. Then I found ThighMaster." When you have a star as your spokesperson, you can count on a significant number of Doubting Thomases who will say, "Oh sure, she looks good. She's got money. She's got a personal trainer." The inclusionary statement diffuses that skepticism. It's like, "Even though I make millions of dollars, my problems are your problems. I'm one of the girls."

The third element required is the authority statement. That's the piece of copy you put in an ad that allows people who *want* to believe in your ad to believe it. In the case of Scope, it was T-70, which is not an active ingredient, mind you; its main attribute was that it sounded scientific. Crest used "fluoristat," which actually referred to something real: fluoride. But fluoristat is a made-up word. The brainchild of a copywriter.

I talked to Josh. Perhaps we could say something about the design of the ThighMaster. He said he would concentrate on the spring. The next day he came into the office. We didn't have any space for him, so he sat on Pippa's couch for a while. When she had to use her office to make some calls, he moved into the conference room. When Joe had to use the conference room for a meeting, he sat on the bench in the reception area.

He was in the office all day. Geez, how hard could it be to write one line? But he took it very seriously.

It was good that he did. By the late afternoon he had it: "The secret to shapely thighs is exercising these muscles with just the right resistance. Too little is ineffective, too much may be painful. This balanced resistance coil is designed to give you results quickly and comfortably."

Balanced resistance coil. *Yes!*

We had to have testimonials, too. They're a crucial part of any infomercial. A testimonial is a sound bite that's pithy. But real people don't talk in sound bites; they ramble. You want them to express themselves in as few words as possible. Short and sweet. Josh gave us the names and telephone numbers of four acquaintances who'd been using the ThighMaster.

Jim took the script through a dozen revisions. You wouldn't think so much brainpower could go into a two-minute spot, but it did. It's the same with conventional advertising, what those of us in direct response call "the other stuff." Per minute, more thought and money goes into television commercials than into the programs. Madison Avenue can spend $300,000 on a 30-second spot, whereas a studio will spend $1 million on an hour-length program like *L.A. Law.* In the 30-second spot, every beat counts—every camera angle, every word, every edit. With a movie or a television drama, you can count on the story to keep people in their seats through the slower passages. The 30-second spot can lose its audience any time to the kitchen or the bathroom.

Meanwhile, I was negotiating Suzanne's contract with Alan. It was like wrestling with an alligator. His negotiating style was win-lose: he wins, you lose. We argued about minimum guarantees, production costs, and her cut of the profits—a lot of things. Every time he returned my call, he'd be on his car phone. If things weren't going his way, if he didn't like what he was hearing, he'd fade out. I'd be left talking to a dial tone. (I know this was deliberate. It's very L.A.)

Also standard practice with Alan was screaming. And yelling obscenities. Boy, could this guy summon up rage. And just when I thought things were settled, he'd bring up four new points—all of them deal-breakers. Never in my life had I negotiated with someone like Alan.

I prayed Suzanne would be worth it.

I started thinking about how we'd shoot the commercial. I knew I wanted to show Suzanne's legs—that's why I'd hired her. A bathing suit or leotard was called for. Jim suggested high heels, which elongate the leg. Then the camera could pan upward until you saw her face. "The legs will hook the viewer. The pan will make you think she's naked. And her face will surprise them," he said gleefully. "People will say, 'Hey, look. That's Suzanne Somers.' "

97

I agreed. But what would the opening line be?

I wanted to open with a voice-over. Maybe I'd use Alan. He could say, "Wow. Great legs. How do you get 'em?"

Yes. I liked that.

Over the next two weeks, I spent time doing two things: fighting with Alan over the phone and setting up the shoot. When the negotiations with Alan looked like they were coming to a conclusion, I chose a shoot date and a location. That done, I hired the director and cameraman, who, between them, would determine the look of the show. I also hired a production manager, Naomi Grossman, whose job it was to see that the project came in on time and on budget.

Then Alan came up with a new set of demands. This started yet *another* round of negotiations and name-calling. I was still confident we'd resolve our disagreements, though, so I continued to finalize the script even as I screamed at Alan over the phone.

But as the shoot date got closer, I started to worry. Without a signed contract, I might end up with a crew of twelve, on location, with nothing to shoot. I gave Alan deadlines but he ignored them. Finally, I was completely out of time. I gave him an ultimatum: Get back to me by 10 A.M. Tuesday or it's over. He promised he'd call.

Tuesday morning, Josh and I were seated in the conference room, staring at the phone. Ten A.M. came and went, and the phone didn't ring. I walked into my office and called the film crew. I got answering machines, so I left messages that the shoot was off. Then I phoned Alan—I got *his* machine, of course, and left the same message. When I hung up, I walked back into the conference room and sat down at the table where I'd spent so many hours over the last month. I couldn't begin to think about how I'd pick up the pieces, who I might hire instead of Suzanne. I stared at the floor.

Just then Leslie walked into the room with a faxed copy of the contract. Signed.

So I phoned all the members of the film crew again, canceling the messages I'd left an hour before. It was a close call.

With the contract signed, I needed to meet with Suzanne to discuss her costume. She asked me to come by her Venice Beach house on Thursday.

Thursday morning I headed out to Marina Peninsula with the costumer. He'd brought some leotards for Suzanne to try on, although she said she had something she could wear.

Suzanne's townhouse sits right on the beach. It's not far from the sweet little canals planned by Abbot Kinney at the turn of the century. (A tobacco tycoon, he had a thing for Venice, Italy. Which is how Venice, California got its name.) Her place is also close to Skatey's Sports, where Randee bought her roller skates, but that's another story.

The house is cream-colored with dark wood trim. There's a floor-to-ceiling window in the living room; a wall of glass, really. A fireplace sits smack in the center of it, obscuring the view of the ocean. The beach is beautiful this far up, and quiet. On this day there were a bunch of people playing volleyball on the sand and a few seagulls hanging around. That was it.

I rang the doorbell, and Alan came down to the garage and led us past the cars and up into the house. He left me in the living room and took the costumer upstairs to Suzanne. (A costumer's job is to make the star feel comfortable with the wardrobe but also to represent the producer's interests in the dressing room. I hoped that he'd nudge her in the direction I wanted her to go.) Alan returned and sat down in front of the brick fireplace. He was so friendly, so cordial. He acted like a harsh word had never passed between us.

Suzanne proceeded with the fashion show. Every ten minutes, she came down the floating staircase, twirled a couple of times, then headed back up to change into another outfit. Forty minutes passed and I still hadn't seen anything resembling a leotard.

"Why don't you put on that little brown thing?" Alan shouted up to her.

Little brown thing? That certainly didn't sound like a leotard.

Sure enough, she came bouncing down the stairs wearing—oh boy, a fuzzy brown suit. It looked like Marian the Librarian's.

"Well, what do you think?" she said, smiling.

"Well, Suzanne," I said, framing my next comment as delicately as possible. "You look great. I mean, you'd look wonderful in a potato sack. But, if you don't mind, I'd really like to see you in one of the leotards I brought. When people reach for a product like ThighMaster, they need to have the results in mind, know what I mean? They need to see your legs. Don't you agree Alan?"

He shrugged his shoulders. It was two against one.

She frowned and went upstairs. When she came back down, she had the leotard on but she didn't look happy. Alan declared that women would be intimidated by it. Besides, he said, it was all wrong for her now. Suzanne nodded gravely. (They were protecting her new image as a serious spokesperson for the children of alcoholics, I guess.) The best I could do was get her to agree that we'd shoot her in both outfits.

We spent one day at a house in the Hollywood Hills, a stone's throw from mine. There, we filmed a sequence of shots—Suzanne using the ThighMaster while watching television, Suzanne using the ThighMaster while talking on the telephone. We worked twelve or thirteen hours. We had lighting directors, caterers, a location manager—about twenty people in all, a small crew by Hollywood standards. Two big grip trucks were parked outside the house. While the crew set up in the living room, Alan and I retired to the den to hash over a few more deal points, which we wrote into the margins of the contract.

Nobody had more at stake than I did, but the day of the shoot I handed the whole enchilada over to the director and production manager. I stood in the wings—in this case, the kitchen—as producers do, biting my nails.

One of the first things we did was shoot the testimonials. These were the people Josh sent us who'd agreed to participate in the infomercial, for free, of course. We talked to them about using ThighMaster and helped them articulate their opinions. We shot four testimonials but used only one. The testimonial we chose was the one from a young woman with "girl next door" appeal. She zips up her jeans, smacks her hips with both hands, and says, grinning broadly, "Thank you, ThighMaster!" She's clearly pleased. We rejected the other three because they came off stiff and insincere.

When it was time to roll the cameras, Suzanne did what stars often do. She got difficult. (I had a feeling this would happen. When we were filming an instructional video for another product, our star's makeup artist looked into the camera and casually commented that the celebrity's nose looked big. No sooner had the words escaped the young woman's lips than the actress stamped off the set and refused to come out of her trailer until we fired the cameraman. Happens all the time.)

Suzanne insisted we shoot the brown suit first. We did. Then she made noises about there not being enough time to shoot the leotard, and besides, the suit looked fine anyway—yada, yada, yada. The director couldn't get her to budge. The man threw up his hands. I stepped in and tried to reason with her. She stood firm; she knew the delay was costing me money. She got her way.

Four days later, I took a look at the rough cut. In a *rough cut*, scenes are strung together without the background music and without the dissolves and the other special effects. I watched the footage in the editing booth.

"Wow. Great legs. How do you get 'em?" said the voiceover. There was the wolf-whistle pan up the legs, which looked gorgeous, and then—*boom*—you hit this woolly skirt. It was *awful*. Not only did it look bad, it raised suspicion. I mean, if you're selling a product that benefits the hips and thighs, you need to see some hips and thighs! It looked like we were hiding something!

We weren't going to sell one ThighMaster with this turkey. (How bad was it? When I showed it to Pippa, she said, "On to the next product.") I had to think fast. Given how tough the negotiations had been, I figured I'd never get Suzanne back on the set to reshoot. I sat down with Pippa and Joe to discuss our options. I had an idea. Maybe we could open with someone else's legs and, halfway up the pan, dissolve to Suzanne's face and hope nobody would notice.

They looked at me like I was nuts.

I was fooling myself. The whole point of the shot was that it was *her,* that the legs were Suzanne Somers' legs.

Bear in mind that I was acutely aware that it had taken longer than I'd expected to get Ovation up and running, that I'd spent Pippa's money faster than I'd anticipated. Yes, there was enough to do another show but it was going to be tight. I really needed this one to work.

There was only one thing to do. I had to get Suzanne back on the set. To do that, I'd have to get her to admit she'd been wrong about the costume. I called her up and told her I wanted to stop by and show her the footage. I knew she'd be anxious to see it. She said to come over on Sunday.

It would be tough going. So I did what any man would do under the circumstances.

I took the wife and kid.

We piled into the car—me, Randee, Holly, who was about eight months old, and Holly's big pink teddy bear. As you already know, my sense of direction is less than stellar. But it's worse when I'm nervous. We ended up driving inland, toward Pomona, which is not the way you get to Venice Beach. It was Randee who noticed we kept heading east. "Are you trying to circumnavigate the globe to get to Venice?" she wisecracked, and told me to just get off the freeway and start all over again. By the time I did this, I was running bloody late. I was a wreck. Worst of all, Holly, normally a mild-mannered baby, was screaming her head off. She was red as a beet. The child *would not* be comforted.

We pulled up to the back of Suzanne's beach house, where we lurched to a stop. Randee quickly combed Holly's hair—all that screaming had worked up a sweat. Holly was wearing this cute little red dress, which complemented her wisps of red hair, but she was sobbing when we walked up to the door.

I rang the bell. Holly stopped crying.

Suzanne answered the door. She was surprised to see Randee and Holly with me, but she greeted us warmly. The baby smiled at her. *What a trouper!* Suzanne took her from Randee, introduced her to Alan, and started cooing and singing to her. It was clear she loved babies. She put her on the carpet with the teddy bear. Holly crawled right back to Suzanne and grabbed her ankle. Suzanne and Alan laughed.

We sat down. Despite Holly's Oscar-winning performance, my insides were churning. Randee smiled tightly.

"So how's it look?" Suzanne asked brightly.

I crossed my legs and flicked an imaginary piece of lint off my knee.

"It's an appealing offer," I began. "The *product* looks good." Her brow furrowed. "But I'm afraid you don't come off as well as I'd hoped, Suzanne."

There. I'd said it.

"We're going to go with it, of course, I just thought you should see it first," I added.

In the time it took to utter the words, I felt a power shift occur. Sure, the ad looked like crap. But it wasn't my face on the tube. It was hers. If she looked ridiculous, it would hurt her more than me, and she knew it.

"Let's have a look," she said solemnly.

We left Randee and Holly and went into the study. Alan slipped the tape into the VCR and flicked the lights off, while Suzanne settled into a big, leather armchair. I pulled up an ottoman. Alan remained standing. I was thinking, if she doesn't agree to reshoot, the fate of the company is in question.

There was the pan up the legs, then Alan's voice, then . . . the hideous skirt.

"We've bought the media time already," I said sotto voce. "We plan to start broadcasting in two weeks, nationally." I was bluffing.

When the tape ended, Alan flicked the lights on and leaned against the back of Suzanne's chair. He said nothing. Suzanne clasped her hands together like she was praying and touched them to her lips. I held my breath.

"Why don't we reshoot using the leotard?" she said suddenly.

"Good idea, Suzanne. I'll have Leslie set it up."

That was it. She made no other comments. She knew she'd been wrong, but she wasn't about to admit it. We returned to the living room, where she kissed Holly and Randee goodbye, and we chatted briefly. I reminded her Leslie would call about setting up another shoot. "See you then, Peter. Drive carefully," she said, and closed the door.

"Whaddya say we get some ice cream?" I asked Randee when we got to the car.

"Okay, but wouldn't you rather have a stiff drink?"

"Nope. It's chocolate raspberry or nothin'."

Holly burped. The vote was unanimous.

CHAPTER · 5

A Virtual
Start Up

***W**ho should direct?*

I'd used seasoned pros for the Gone shoot and the ThighMaster shoot, and things still went badly. I began to consider directing the second ThighMaster shoot myself. Mind you, I had a lot of ambivalence about it. Randee quipped that I must be the only reluctant director in Hollywood. (I'm reminded of a joke about Mother Teresa. A reporter interviews her, praising her tireless work with the poor; her devotion to the sick, the orphaned, and the outcast. "Yes," she replies, "but what I really want to do is *direct.*")

True, I came from the film business and had worked under some of the best directors in town—Peter Yates, Franco Zeffirelli—people with a tremendous capacity for visualization. But that didn't mean I was prepared to direct. I kept thinking about something John McTiernan's ex-wife, Carol, told me. (Carol was my VP marketing.) Carol said that when John was asked to explain his unique talent for coordinating chase scenes, explosions, and other technical feats, he said that he saw the movie projected on the back of his eyelids. Granted, directing a short-form infomercial was one step up from a slide show compared to directing *The Hunt for Red October* or *Die Hard,* to name two of John's films, but hey, it was still production. It required, albeit to a lesser degree, this ability to see a scene with your mind's eye before a single foot of film is shot. (The primary responsibility of a director is the placement of the camera. The camera represents the viewer's eye.) I wasn't sure I could pull it off.

I telephoned Randee's writing partner, Laurie Craig. Laurie's a screenwriter and a director. I told her that I wanted a smooth transition between jump cuts in the opening montage but that I wasn't sure how that might be accomplished. I was also worried about plotting the camera angles. Would she help me? Sure, she said.

Laurie was great. I couldn't have done it without her.

In the meantime, I received a videotape in the mail from Alan and Suzanne. There was a note enclosed. It read: "Here's what we have in mind for the reshoot. Enjoy!" Hmph. Obviously they didn't trust my vision for the commercial.

What they'd done was take a camcorder to the beach and get creative. There was Suzanne, sitting up against the wall of her Venice beach house, speaking earnestly about ThighMaster. It was a serious, woman-to-woman chat. There was no sex appeal, no humor. The content was all wrong.

I called Alan and told him I was willing to give something like that a try, but I insisted we do it my way first. (When the day of the shoot came, we shot it both ways. Alan directed their version, of course, but it was never edited. Once they saw mine they knew we had a winner.)

As you already know, for the first shoot we'd spent a day at a house in the Hollywood Hills. For the second shoot, I rented the small stage at Landsburg, the one where Tony Hoffman's *Everybody's Money Matters* had been shot. (It may sound like this was the only insert stage in Hollywood. It's not. It was just handy for me.) The crew was smaller than before, consisting of a camera-man/lighting director, two grips, a boom man, audio and video control, a production manager, me and maybe three other people. We used minimal lights. For background we used a roll of blue paper. This was where we filmed the opening where Suzanne, wearing high heels, a leotard, and a kleig-light smile, kicks off the sales pitch.

We started at 8 A.M. Suzanne struck the right attitude—half tease, half "I'm in on the joke, too." Her performance was over the top; a sex symbol doing an impression of a sex symbol. (Marilyn Monroe was an expert at this.) The effect, of course, was engaging. It always is when the real person pokes fun at his or her own persona. (George Hamilton has built a career on doing a send-up of George Hamilton. Ditto for Liberace.) As it happens, Suzanne has a lively sense of humor, too, which proved invaluable when it came time to promote the product on talk shows. In *Quotable Business,* where she's sandwiched between Jean Paul Getty and Charles Baudelaire, she says in reference to all the TV shows she shot that went nowhere: "When people asked me what I did for a living, I told them, 'I do pilots.' They all thought I was a stewardess." That's Suzanne.

We did several takes until I was satisfied with what I saw in the monitor. Then we moved on.

I'd already decided to make the commercial sexier. I'd hired my aerobics instructor for the shot where the balanced resistance coil is explained. Though important from a marketing standpoint, the voiceover is dull stuff. What you see on the screen, though, is a lithesome woman lying on the floor, exercising with ThighMaster.

I also shot an attractive couple to demonstrate the upper-body benefits of ThighMaster. They were plucked from L.A.'s vast pool of "beautiful people for hire," the sometime-models and would-be actors who, more often than not, end up keeping their day jobs. The two had been romantically involved and were in the process of becoming uninvolved. There were icy looks and snide remarks, but when the camera started rolling they were all smiles. Pippa told me to have the woman admire her bicep as she pumped the ThighMaster. It came off sexy. A nice bit of direction.

All went well and without incident until about 4 P.M., when news about the bombing of Baghdad began to spread. It was January 16, 1991, and Desert Storm had begun. There was a television on in the wardrobe room, and as the evening wore on, people drifted back and forth between the TV and the stage. I was one of them. It was an eerie feeling to be at war. Stranger still was to be at war while filming a two-minute spot. In the middle of a discussion about lighting and makeup, the props master came running over to tell us that NBC had reported that no American jets had been shot down.

At 6, we broke for dinner and listened to President Bush's address to the nation. By 9 P.M., the crew was packing up, the film was in the can, and I'd spent another $20,000.

What a sense of relief! But it didn't last long. Now I had the testing process to look forward to.

Every morning on the way to the office I stopped at the Butterfly on Westwood Boulevard. Liz's Butterfly Bakery. It's the kind of place where a cop can go behind the counter and pour a cup of coffee. But there aren't any donuts. Westwood cops snack on scones or bran muffins. Stars drop in all the time, too. Big stars. Their autographed photos hang on the walls.

This particular morning, I was sitting beneath Rodney Danger-field and Burgess Meredith, making a list of the kinds of companies with which I needed to contract to form what ultimately would become—if a test succeeded—a virtual corporation.

I would need to outsource all the functions of a conventional marketing company—buying media time, taking orders, processing orders, shipping orders, and manufacturing product. My first order of business was to hire a media agency.

As I've since learned to appreciate, hiring a media agency is a major decision. You're going to live with that agency throughout the test period and, most likely, for the duration of the campaign's rollout.

First and foremost, by all means, hire an agency that specializes in direct-response marketing. Besides the obvious benefits, media agencies specializing in direct response own a lot of media time. They either sell it or trade it with other agencies. It's to your advantage to be part of that consortium. Such agencies also tend to specialize in either long-form or short-form. Make your choice accordingly.

The big telemarketing firms are based in Omaha. Why? Because Omaha is one of the most wired cities in America, thanks to the Department of Defense. When the underground headquarters for the Strategic Air Command moved to Omaha, Northwestern Bell beefed up the telecircuitry. There's just tremendous capacity. As a result, Omaha became a major hotel and car-rental reservation center. Its location in the central time zone provided an economic advantage, too, since 800 numbers used to be distance-sensitive. (That's no longer the case.) And the operators have Midwestern, that is, neutral accents.

It's important that you go with a large telemarketer. With a national TV campaign, there are incredible peaks in order volume during and immediately following the airing of a commercial. Customers who get a busy signal aren't likely to phone back. Direct-response campaigns running close to breakeven can be sunk by inadequate inbound telemarketing capabilities.

It's important to choose a credit-card processing company that can work closely with your telemarketer. And the choices are limited, as only a few processors in the country are set up to handle credit-card transactions where there's no signed receipt. These companies also authorize credit-card purchases before product is shipped; in other words, they make certain the credit card is valid and that adequate credit is available for the purchase. Then they deposit the receipts in your merchant account and wire you the money daily. They also make multiple charges against your customers' cards for offers with payment plans (as in "Three easy payments of $19.95!").

Fulfillment houses stock your product. They take authorized orders from the credit-card processor, box them, label them, and put them on a UPS truck. They also deal with customer inquiries about lost shipments and handle returns (examining the product, issuing credits, and the like).

I knew it was my responsibility to identify suppliers that would do each of these jobs and negotiate good rates with them. I also had to make sure they'd worked with each other before: I didn't want to be a trailblazer in setting up communications. With a virtual corporation, you can't depend on the shipping guy to bump into the data processing guy at the water cooler: They're not under one roof. You need to make sure all the companies are tied together in a tightly knit electronic network with a daily and dependable flow of information. A virtual corporation will sink into bankruptcy without this dependable electronic network. Bear in mind that, at the time I was making my list at the Butterfly, the Internet was difficult to access. Now it's easier than ever to tie these disparate entities together.

The last element I needed was a factory. I knew I had a small but adequate inventory of product for a test. I would have enough time *after* the test to look for a manufacturer before rolling out the campaign.

Let's talk about the importance of testing. As with conventional advertising, the testing process in direct response is about learning if your ad is effective. But there's a big difference. In direct response, a test is a trial run. You ask people to make a purchase. You want to determine how effectively your commercial attracts *orders*. Mainstream advertisers test the *appeal* of an ad. They show it to a focus group, say, twenty homemakers in Peoria, and ask them if they'd buy the product. Or they ask them to fill out a questionnaire on the way into the supermarket.

A direct-response test is infinitely more precise. You can find out if you're making money on every transaction, right from the start. Conventional advertisers spend $5 million and look for a bump in the sales curve five months down the road. Direct-response advertisers who spend $1,000 on a half hour here or there know how many orders they need to see to make the ad pay out. And a test tells them if they're reaching that target.

If you don't avail yourself of a test, you've given up the biggest safety net direct response offers. By all means, air the ad in a half dozen test markets and see if a specifically determined number of phones light up after each broadcast. They either ring or they don't. Pass, fail.

Now the purpose of the test is to determine a cost, a highly variable cost, that means the difference between success and failure. And that's how much of your revenue you have to set aside to pay for media time. You can go into a campaign knowing the cost of everything but the cost of air time, and it could be fully 50 percent of your revenue if the product tests well.

The calculation is simple and the answer either sweet or brutal depending on the results. Let's say you spend $1,000 to buy one run on a single broadcast station in Los Angeles, and that broadcast makes the phone ring 120 times, producing 100 orders. (The rest were just crank calls and inquiring minds.) That means that $10 out of every order is spent paying for the media. (The $1000 media purchase divided by 100 orders.) Probably profitable on a $20 product. You should expect to spend about 50% of your revenue on media.

Now, let's say the phones ring only 80 times, producing 70 orders. Now you're spending over $14 out of every order on media. That doesn't leave enough to cover all of the other costs and expected profit. So the campaign is a failure.

This crucial figure is called the *CPO,* or cost per order, and it's the figure all the fuss is about. (Other costs, such as manufacturing and shipping, can be assessed well before the test.) Cost per order can apply to a single broadcast or an entire campaign. Direct marketers look at their CPOs every morning but never with more interest than during a test run. With a $10,000 media purchase for a six-city test and a $20 product, you're looking for about a thousand orders. But you're also looking at your test results market by market, which is to say, broadcast by broadcast.

About the mechanics of testing:

First, you test the concept with about $10,000. If it clicks, you roll out and head for the bank. If your CPO is 200 percent over your target, like it was with Gone, America does not want your product. Look for another one. If you're in the ballpark, say, 15 to 20 percent over your target, you're on to a second stage, where you'll want to alter the elements of your offer, along with the creative and the media plan, to strengthen the appeal of your commercial, and retest. It's not unusual for this process to cost an additional $40,000 in media. But beware of agencies that demand $35,000 to $50,000 going in to test an ad over a two-to-three-week period. Don't go along with it. Always insist on stretching out the testing process so you can make changes between airings or cancel your bookings without penalty if the test results are hopeless and you can't improve the show.

You also need to be sure that the mix of cities represents the nation as a whole. I believe in a mix of one-third cable networks and two-thirds broadcast stations. The broadcast stations should be spread across the country, in cities of all sizes, and across time zones, too, unless it's a regional product like a fishing lure. Beware of test schedules where there are multiple broadcasts in New Haven or West Palm Beach. There isn't anything that doesn't sell in New Haven (no one knows why), and as for West Palm Beach, maybe it's the proximity to millionaires that drives the middle class into a buying frenzy. Good results are guaranteed in these cities, so they're unreliable test markets.

Because you want to measure the success of each television broadcast, every station has a different phone number—WTMV in Tampa, KTVX in Salt Lake City—so you will know how many orders each broadcast has delivered. Then you can calculate profitability by station, time of day, city, whatever you want to know. It is common for a campaign to have a successful CPO in some markets and not in others. That's why media schedules are changed weekly and sometimes daily. You're dropping the markets that don't work and picking up others that hopefully will.

We contracted with West Telemarketing, based in Omaha. Imagine a cavernous room filled with up to five hundred people—retired people, college freshmen, but mostly homemakers—all of them sitting in cubicles, wearing headsets and staring at computer screens. There's the low hum of conversation. Each operator handles twenty-five to thirty calls an hour. They take orders not only for direct-response products but also for catalogue items and the myriad of novelties advertised in the back pages of magazines. The computer sorts out all the different accounts.

For its direct-response clients who are running tests, the telemarketing company tabulates the results instantaneously, so you can phone in any time you want during the test weekend to get the latest figures broken down by test market.

I'd been through this nightmare of waiting and calling, waiting and calling, with the Gone test. Here I was again, sitting home all weekend, reaching for the phone twenty minutes after every broadcast.

Gone notwithstanding, most shows test neither as hits nor as failures. The ThighMaster ad did so-so. The CPO was coming in 20 percent higher than where I needed it to be to be profitable. Not great, but close enough that some minor adjustments could make it work. Adjustments that didn't require reshooting.

What constitutes minor adjustments? Well, you might go back into the editing room and change the music or edit a scene that drags. You could adjust your media plan, emphasizing one part of the country over another, or cable over broadcast, or large cities over small cities, or weekend days versus weekday overnights, or many other possibilities. It's truly remarkable how a show that plays strong in Seattle can tank in New Orleans.

But the element you should pay the most attention to when fixing a show is the offer. The offer includes payment plan, guarantee, upsell (the second item the nice lady in Omaha tries to sell you when you call to place your order), price, and premiums. The offer is the most overlooked yet significant ingredient in a successful infomercial.

American Telecast has had more big hits in terms of gross revenues than any company in the infomercial business, largely because of its innovative offers. Though Cher was inspired casting for a line of hair-care products, the Lori Davis infomercial (yes, the one spoofed on *Saturday Night Live*) owes much of its success to an innovative payment plan. When customers called in to place an order, they were encouraged to become members in a club.

Why would they join? Well, the product was cheaper for members, and every seventh month you got a free shipment. Their credit cards were charged monthly until they said no—what's known in the business as a *negative response* campaign. It's precisely what the Book-of-the-Month Club does. To stop the charges you have to call them off.

Such an offer supports continuing use of the product because (1) you look forward to getting something in the mail every month; (2) there's no buying decision—your credit card is charged automatically; and (3) it's easier to keep getting the stuff than to go to the trouble of stopping it.

Can tweaking an offer make a big difference? Absolutely. Connie Selleca and John Tesh were celebrity hosts in the *Hidden Keys to Loving Relationships* series. After their show hit the air, American Telecast did not get the CPO it was looking for. So the offer was changed. The price of the first video tape was dropped to $9.95, though subsequent tapes were mailed out monthly at $24.95 each. Sales zoomed. People couldn't resist what they perceived as a bargain. Same script, same hosts. Only the payment plan was altered.

For her skin-care products, Victoria Principal offered her "bottom-of-the-jar" guarantee. Just send it back. No matter how much you used, she'd refund your money. (Bear in mind that this is not quite as bold an offer as it may sound, because most people don't bother to return products through the mail unless they really hate them or they arrive broken. It's too much of a hassle.) Principal's creative guarantee was designed to generate sales. It reinforced the feeling that you were getting something on a trial basis. Why *not* pick up the phone?

Many campaigns depend on the profitability of upsell. This is particularly true of lower-priced products, those under $50. Normally 20 percent of the people who call to order an infomercial product go for the upsell item. When people phoned to buy Thigh-Master, they were offered the ThighMaster Total Body Toning video for $14.95. Twenty percent went for the offer.

Let's turn to pricing. Products offered on long-form shows are generally priced at $29.95 or higher. How much higher? Jane Fonda's Fitness Tread was priced at $359.46, Gravity Edge (with host Lorenzo Lamas) was priced at $399.95, and the ProForm Cross Trainer (with hosts Peggy Fleming and Roger Staubach) went for a staggering $799.95. All of these shows were big hits. Although multi-payment plans are common at this level, these buyers are hardly Goodwill regulars.

The majority of short-form products are priced at $19.95 or less. We tested ThighMaster at $19.95 and $29.95, and both prices worked: We sold plenty of product. But $19.95 worked on *every* TV station we ran it on. This was important. I wanted a campaign that could run everywhere because I planned to go retail. Maximizing the number of people who saw my commercial was as important to me as maximizing profits from direct response. The fact that we had to sell three ThighMasters at $19.95 for every one we sold for $29.95 to make the same profit was secondary. The golden goose was the brand awareness that would result from massive TV exposure.

But before we were successful, we had to add a premium to motivate them to phone ("Call now and get the carrying case for free! Call now and we'll send you this beautiful picture frame!"). In our first test, we didn't include this basic building block of direct-response success, and I suspect it was the reason our CPO was unprofitably high.

A premium serves two purposes: It fills out the offer—you get more for your money—and it also allows you to address any concerns in the viewer's mind. We were showing these fabulous benefits—Suzanne's gorgeous legs, the sexy couple, the svelte aerobics instructor and, well, our promise seemed a little too good to be true. Everybody knows you don't lose weight from exercise alone. You have to watch what you eat, too. *How could you look that good without dieting?* (The ad says ThighMaster tones and strengthens, but there's not one word about burning calories. It does, of course but not enough to position it as a weight reducer.)

The solution? The Suzanne Somers Slender-for-Life Plan, a four-page diet menu plan for losing weight. (The doctor who headed the weight-loss clinic at the famed La Costa health spa and resort helped us put it together.) The menu was mentioned at the end of the commercial, and *bang*—more phones started ringing and our CPO fell. We had a successful test.

The premium made the offer more credible. People didn't believe they could get the results they wanted without also dieting; the menu plan addressed a *real* concern. It didn't push people toward the phone so much as clear the path for them. This is not to say that more is always better. The gratuitous use of premiums does not assure success. An offer is analogous to a house of cards. Every aspect of it, like every card, is there for a reason.

But I didn't tell a soul about our test results. Knock-offs are a major problem in this business. You have a hit, and boom, an imitator siphons off your sales, and in some cases, infringes on your patent. It's fast, easy money. And the knock-offs are as likely to come from established companies as from shady characters on the fringe. Smart Mop got knocked off by E-Z Mop, Health-Rider got knocked off by CardioGlide. Perfect Smile got knocked off by Dental White. A slew of knock-offs saturated the juicer market a few years ago. So, throughout the test period, it's essential that you swear yourself and your media agency to secrecy.

Once you have your test results, you can gauge rather accurately how successful you'll be in a rollout. It's like a Gallup poll, where the temper of 270 million Americans is gauged by talking to only 2,000 or 3,000 of us. Spending $25,000 in media for carefully selected markets, you can tell what kind of results you'll get if you spend $200,000 a week across the country. But as any politician can tell you, poll results aren't a prediction. They're an indication. I still had a lot of work to do.

Like rolling out the campaign. I figured I'd stick with the media-buying agency I was using.

We were a brand-new company, remember, not American Telecast or Quantum. So we didn't have any credit. Of necessity we had gone with a media agency that was willing to buy the time and resell it to us. At the time, we used the direct-response division of a behemoth media operation here in Los Angeles.

There was just one problem. I didn't know it, but our media agency's direct-response subsidiary handled 900 numbers. That meant phone sex. While the parent company was buying air time for Fortune 500 companies, "respectable" clients, the direct-response division was catering to companies employing women with a talent for feigning orgasm while buffing their nails.

Now, the challenge with party lines and phone sex is not making profitable media buys, it's finding a station that will run your ad. A lot of TV stations refuse to air them. So the pool of stations our agency was doing business with was small.

I phoned the agency every week, *begging* them to spend my money, to *please* buy me time on some more stations. "I'm sitting on a gold mine, guys! Buy, buy!" I'd yell into the receiver. But there was always some lame excuse. It was extraordinarily frustrating. Why couldn't we get into more markets?

The fortunate side to this dilemma was that it gave me time to get my ducks in order. For starters, to get staffed up. I'd been wanting to hire Mike Clark, for example. Like me, Mike had worked in the motion picture business. Then he went to law school at night and worked as a media buyer during the day at one of the first advertising agencies to buy air time for infomercials, the Donald D. Lewis agency. Lewis had bought time for a slew of early infomercial hits, including Albert J. Lowry's real-estate seminars and Tony Hoffman's *Everybody's Money Matters.* From there, Mike's career took off. He had an impressive resume.

I knew that hiring Mike signaled a change. Jumping to 10,000 units a week in direct response would mean staffing up like crazy. It meant customer services; an MIS department; a comptroller, an accountant, and bookkeepers; print and electronic creative services; manufacturing and inventory; personnel; and, to go retail, client services and sales. Ovation was about to take off.

Yet there was something odd about it. I was feeling nostalgic for something I hadn't lost yet. I imagined it was like those hours or days before you cash in a multimillion-dollar lottery ticket. You know your life's about to change irrevocably, that reporters will be calling and cameras will be flashing, and you want to savor the last few moments of normalcy, of calm.

It was time to visit Marilyn.

Westwood Village Memorial Park was right behind my building. Indeed, I had a full view of its tree-shaded lawn from my office window. The little cemetery was built in 1905, which explained its unlikely presence in the heart of a business district. Darryl F. Zanuck, John Cassavetes, Natalie Wood, Truman Capote, and many others are buried there.

Its most popular denizen is Marilyn Monroe. She's tucked inside a granite wall with a bunch of other people. There's always a pile of cards, baskets of flowers, and a clutch of balloons on the ground below her simple bronze plaque. The tributes are from around the world, but the sentiments are the same—we love you, we miss you, we'll always remember you. It's quite touching. I often had lunch on the bench near Marilyn when I needed quiet and some space.

As I sat there with my chicken salad and bottle of Snapple, I reflected on the sea of change about to come. There would be fewer free weekends, which meant less time with Randee and Holly; no time to read and to travel, my two favorite pastimes; more late nights and more sleepless nights. Dreamily I considered what my life would be like if I didn't ride the comet. We could easily sell 2,500 to 3,500 ThighMasters a week for years to come. A $3-million-a-year business. A nice living.

Yeah, but not a fit ending to *this* movie. There was never any doubt I was going for broke. I wiped my mouth with a napkin and headed back to the office, humming softly.

I called Mike Clark and hired him. The following day I fired my sex-line media agency and hired another, this one in New York. The numbers went crazy.

In direct response, the size of a hit is defined in two ways: the number of markets in which your show runs profitably *and* the show's ability to work well around the clock. ThighMaster was a colossal hit by both definitions.

It worked everywhere. All the time.

Within weeks, we went from selling 2,000 ThighMasters a week to selling 7,500. Within five months, we were shipping 75,000 a week. After 24 months, we'd sold 6 million.

While orders were going through the roof, we were still using the limited operation in Chicago that manufactured the prototype for

Josh and the 500 ThighMasters I'd used for the test. I had to find a real factory.

I was looking for a jobber in Phoenix because that's where our fulfillment house was located. Gary Gibby was referred to me.

Gibby, I was told, could make anything. He was one of those guys who, if your car broke down in the middle of nowhere, could get it going again with a pair of needle-nosed pliers, some dental floss, and a nail file. If he had to, I'll bet he could fieldstrip a B-17.

By the time we met, he'd already seen the ThighMaster. Someone in my office had sent it to him. I'd also checked his references. They were excellent.

I found him leaning back in one of those old metal desk chairs in a tiny office with a dirty window overlooking the plant floor. He offered me a seat on a broken-down couch. (It was clear he hadn't spent a dime on interior decoration, that all his money was tied up in tools and machinery.) He had thick arms and a barrel chest. His face was weather-beaten, baked dry by the Arizona sun.

I asked him what the guys on the plant floor were doing. Painting plastic cases for computers, he replied gruffly. Silence followed. So much for small talk.

The ThighMaster was sitting on his desk. It was the only colorful object in his office, and it looked strangely out of place, like a vase of flowers in a gas station.

"So, you think you can make this thing?" I said, gesturing to the ThighMaster.

He put his Styrofoam coffee cup down and reached across the desk, the springs of his chair squeaking with every movement. He picked up the ThighMaster and gave it a few rapid squeezes.

"Yeah," he snorted, "I can make it," and dropped it on the desk.

I told him the first order was for 20,000 but that if we agreed to do business it would be on a trial basis. If the product looked good, felt good, and passed quality control, then we'd have a deal. Before I left his office, he shook my hand. I swear I heard my knuckles crunching.

Gary geared up quickly, putting the ThighMasters through their paces. He designed and built some testing equipment of his own and we later backed him up with an industrial test lab in Los

Angeles. When we were both satisfied with what came off the assembly line, I gave him another order. Then another.

Gary never anticipated the volume he'd have to handle. I think he figured he'd make a couple hundred thousand of the things, tops. Within four months, there were two hundred people assembling ThighMasters. The factory was busy around the clock. For a few months, there were twenty to thirty semi-trailers parked in front of the plant, waiting to be loaded.

Gary's computer-painting business fell by the wayside.

Back in Westwood, things were getting complicated. We had a far-flung operation. There was the manufacturing plant in Phoenix, the inbound telephone operation in Omaha, the credit-card processing company we'd contracted with in Salem, New Hampshire, the media agency in New York, the fulfillment house in Nashville (we had to switch to a larger warehouse than the one in Phoenix). We were outsourcing everything. The term *virtual corporation* was hardly being used at the time, but that's what we had: a decentralized, networked organization of independent companies which could be called on to focus their energies on a single campaign. It was precisely the kind of structure a lot of companies are striving to achieve through "reengineering."

Where traditional companies have divisions, we had independent contractors, each with its own way of doing things. Joe Grace kept this network of diverse companies focused on a single goal. It was an important part of his job as COO in charge of day-to-day operations.

The definition of a virtual corporation is not that it outsources most of its functions—every company outsources *something*—but rather that the core company's functions are so few. In fact, there are often just three: product development, marketing, and distribution. This was true of Ovation.

Though the core company had swelled to forty employees, Ovation was hardly a large, vertically integrated company.

Good thing, too. Everybody knows start-up entrepreneurs make lousy managers and fail to make the transition successfully, Bill Gates being a notable exception. The skills needed to launch a company are very different than those required to run a vertically integrated company. Entrepreneurs are used to doing everything themselves, a destructive habit in a traditional, hierarchical organization.

The nice thing about a virtual corporation is that you don't have to change. You don't have to transform yourself from a frontline manager to a guy that sits at the top of a huge pyramid of employees. You have a better chance of succeeding because the skills that got you there will keep you there. You can grow rather large, yet keep your start-up mentality.

The other advantage to a virtual structure is that you can grow rapidly. As any businessman will tell you, the scarcest resource is skilled labor. The risk and expense of searching out and recruiting personnel, not to mention the drain on executive time, is enormous for a fast-growing company. You also avoid the expense of training new recruits. Ovation didn't have a training program of any consequence; we contracted with suppliers who had staff in place.

Not only can you grow rapidly, you can shrink—painlessly—if need be. The companies in a virtual corporation are like freelance writers—they finish one project and go on to another. They don't need the core company to survive. You sign a contract with them or you don't. There's no such thing as scrambling for employees during upswings and big layoffs during downcycles.

We didn't face the capital demands of most start-ups either. Most young companies in any industry fail because they're undercapitalized. They have to spend money on training programs, on setting up systems, on capital goods like machinery—all before they see the fruits of their labor. Instead, we were free to focus our financial resources on inventory growth. After all, if you sell three widgets today, you gotta manufacture four tomorrow.

We were free to spend money to make money.

Here's another advantage to a virtual corporation. When something goes wrong in a vertically integrated company, a new procedure is written. But in too many cases, these very procedures make it harder to get the job done. Employees are less efficient because of paperwork, rules, and so on. Procedures also stifle ingenuity.

The beauty of a network of small companies tied together in a virtual corporation is that the boss is close to the frontline decisions. There's an operating *intelligence,* not an operating *manual.* Again, we had Gary Gibby solving problems, not some guy following ossified procedures in a dusty manufacturing manual. We had top-flight people solving our credit-card processing problems, not some low-level employee scared to do something creative out of fear of losing his job.

For so many reasons, the structure of a virtual corporation makes sense. And cents.

By September 1991, ThighMasters were selling like crazy on television. We'd also been selling them in booths at county and state fairs across the country, a sizable market frequently overlooked by direct-response advertisers. The Los Angeles County Fair, a major event, runs for three weeks in September and attracts 1.5 million people. We had three booths set up, all of them managed by Bill Heichert, who'd hired the salespeople.

One Saturday night I got a telephone call at home from Bill. He said somebody was selling something called a Thigh Magic at the fair; that they had three booths, just like we did; that their product looked a lot like the ThighMaster, only it was a different color. Worse yet, they were selling it for less. They were hurting our business.

"I think you got a knock-off problem, Peter," sighed Bill. "Better call a lawyer."

A knock-off problem? Call a lawyer?

Shit. I hung up and yelled for Randee.

CHAPTER · 6

Ambushed

The next morning, Heichert stopped by the house and dropped off a Thigh Magic. He'd bought one after we hung up, knowing I'd be anxious to see it. It looked a lot like the ThighMaster, only the foam handles were black and the plastic cap over the spring was pink. The ThighMaster in drag.

As I turned it over in my hands, I realized I was looking at the possibility of my whole media campaign being derailed. We'd been advertising heavily for three to four months, and America was starting to pay attention. I was buying a lot of media and I needed a lot of direct-response sales to pay for it. If a competitor started siphoning off my customers, I'd be faced with taking the campaign off the air. Goodbye national advertising, goodbye retail, goodbye dream. I felt sick to my stomach just thinking about it.

After Bill left, we got Holly washed and dressed. The Bieler family was going to the fair.

Along the way, we stopped at Radio Shack, where I bought a tiny tape recorder with a built-in microphone. Our mission was to visit the Thigh Magic booth and record whatever incriminating things the salespeople were saying. (I had some vague understanding that it was okay to tape-record people in public, that it wasn't illegal.) I didn't know what incriminating *meant,* of course—I was completely untutored in these things—but I felt I had to do something, that I had to take some action. Randee was game.

When we got to the fair, we set about securing the tape recorder to Holly's stroller. Randee hid it in the folds of the hood. I set the record volume on high and tested it a few times to make sure it was picking up voices. While we fussed with the tape recorder, Holly chortled and played with her toes.

We walked around until we found one of the three Thigh Magic booths, where several good-looking women in pink hot pants were selling the product. They must have been paid by commission because they were working real hard. The minute we stopped at the booth, they pounced on us.

PERKY BLONDE [*Stooping over baby*]: "Oh, she's *so* adorable. What's her name? *Holly?* That's *such* a pretty name. Well, you don't need a Thigh Magic, sweetie. [*Turning toward Randee*] "But, hey, Mom, what about you?"

"That's a really neat-looking product," said Randee, without skipping a beat. "Tell me about it." The blonde sat down, put the Thigh Magic between her knees, and started demonstrating—all the while going on about how easy it was to use and how it was *just like the Suzanne Somers thing on television, only better and cheaper.*

That was all I needed. I elbowed Randee, and she muttered something about our having to catch up with some friends, and we split. We searched out the other two booths and collected similar statements on tape. When we returned to the car, I took the microcassette out of the recorder and dropped it into my shirt pocket. "Mission accomplished," I said to Randee. "We've got the goods."

On Monday I contacted the law firm of Venable, Baetjer, Howard & Civiletti in Washington, D.C. One of its partners, Jeff Knowles, had helped form the then-year-old National Infomercial Marketing Association, created to lend some respectability to the upstart industry. (Knowles continues to serve as NIMA's general counsel.) The firm had attorneys who specialized in intellectual property litigation, but, more importantly, they understood the infomercial business, thanks to Knowles' involvement with NIMA. These were the guns to hire.

Jim Myers, a top intellectual-property litigator in the firm, wasn't available, so I met with Ed Glynn, a Venable lawyer who'd spent the better part of his career at the Federal Trade Commission. He was born in Boston but grew up in Montreal, where his family had a baked-goods packaging company. He had a sharp wit and an Irish mug. Give him a uniform and a badge and he'd look like a cop on a Stephen Bochco series.

I told Ed that Josh Reynolds had applied for a design patent for the ThighMaster, which we hoped to see issued in about six months. And I knew that, in the interim, we could print PATENT PENDING on our boxes, which would give us the right to sue people down the line if they infringed. That's about all I knew, except that most direct-response products didn't have patents because patents take so long to get and most infomercial marketers are selling products they have licensed and are rushing to market. We were ahead of most folks.

Ed drew a deep breath and explained the basics of patent law. There are two kinds of patents, he said: design patents, which protect the decorative or ornamental elements of a product, and utility patents, which protect the functional attributes of a product. A design patent is considerably easier to obtain than a utility patent, he noted, reminding me that that's what we had in the wings. He emphasized that it was important to have applied for the right patent because the other side's attorney will always argue that you've applied for the wrong one.

Ed told me that, until our patent was issued, our only hope was to claim trade-dress infringement. Trade dress, Ed explained, can protect a product pending a patent from knock-offs.

To qualify for trade-dress protection, a product has to be highly recognizable by the general public, because the point of trade dress is to protect consumers from being confused and mistakenly buying a look-alike instead of the real thing. The ThighMaster was already identifiable; people knew what it was the minute they saw one. This meant nobody had the right to come along and confuse the public with a knock-off.

Knock-offs I knew about. Mike Clark had already explained to me the difference between a knock-off and a counterfeit. A knock-off, he said, is a product that resembles the original but has a different name, say, Molex instead of Rolex. It's a cheap alternative to the real thing. A counterfeit, by contrast, is a product that tries to pass itself off *as the real thing.* A "Rolex" watch sold out of a suitcase in front of Bergdorf Goodman on Fifth Avenue is undoubtedly counterfeit.

After a few telephone conversations, we decided to file motion papers in federal district court in Los Angeles seeking a temporary restraining order, which would allow us to raid the knock-off people and seize their product, supplies, and records. In addition, Ed asked for the moon and the stars. He requested an ex parte decision, which meant the Thigh Magic folks would be caught by surprise, red-handed, if you will. And finally, Ed asked for the right to use all reasonable force, which meant we could get the marshalls to break down their doors, if necessary, like DEA agents in a drug bust. Submitted with the motion papers was an affidavit about the comments I'd heard in the booths at the fair. (I knew that tape would come in handy!)

The matter was assigned to U.S. District Judge Terry J. Hatter, Jr. (Hatter is the judge who, two years later, temporarily derailed the Clinton Administration's carefully negotiated "don't ask, don't tell" policy with a ruling that banned discrimination against homosexuals in the military.)

I learned that to win a trade-dress suit you've got to prove that the product's design is fanciful *and* that the public recognizes your product. Ordinarily, you hire a testing firm to gather consumer survey evidence. The firm places people in shopping malls—mall intercepts, they're called—who stop shoppers and ask them if they've ever seen this product and if they can identify it.

But we didn't have time to do that. So we attached to the motion papers, all the videotapes and transcripts from *The Tonight Show with Jay Leno, The Arsenio Hall Show, Late Night with David Letterman,* and so on. The ThighMaster was garnering a lot of attention by then, and was fodder for comedians. It was also popping up in movies and sitcoms. (Our PR campaign was memorable and I discuss it in Chapter 8.) It was pretty obvious, we felt, that these Thigh Magic guys were getting a free ride on our publicity.

To my amazement, we got a response the same day. One of Hatter's law clerks telephoned Ed that the judge had signed the order exactly as it was presented to him.

Talk about fast action. It took more time to get my driver's license renewed than to get a court order. Even Ed was astonished. What was all this stuff about the wheels of justice turning slower than a pig on a spit?

The court order directed the United States Marshall Service to seize all the Thigh Magics in the booths at the Los Angeles County Fair and at the assembly site; to seize business documents sufficient to demonstrate how many Thigh Magics had been sold and how much money had been made; and it prevented the sale of further Thigh Magics by stopping all work.

Judge Hatter also set a court date 10 days later for a preliminary injunction hearing. At that hearing, we'd have to make a much fuller accounting of their infraction. If we prevailed, we would have the right to continue to hold their product and supplies until a full trial could be set. If we lost, we'd have to give them back their product and records, and they could continue doing business unfettered.

The coordination of the raids was a thing of beauty—well, from my point of view, anyway. Federal marshalls simultaneously descended on the three booths at the fair and a house in the San Fernando Valley where the Thigh Magics were being assembled. At the fair, the marshalls entered through the front and the back of the booths so that no one could flee with product. The models in hot pants were blown away; they couldn't believe what was happening. In the face of seizure warrants, there was nothing to do but go home.

The raid in the Valley was even more exciting. The large white house belonged to Peter Breitinger, who was home at the time. His partner, Brian MacGregor, was out picking up raw materials. Breitinger and MacGregor operated out of flea markets and county fairs; on the fringe, so to speak. Breitinger, a hard-driving veteran of the pitch business had made millions manufacturing and selling a plastic doo-dad that allowed you to pile a lot of clothes on one hanger. MacGregor, clean-cut and boyish-looking, was from Milwaukee and had a background in marketing and distribution. They had about thirty people working for them in Breitinger's backyard, putting together thousands of Thigh Magics under tents. When the federal marshalls arrived, the workers, who may have mistaken them for INS agents, took off like rabbits.

Breitinger resisted at first. He knew we didn't have a patent yet, so he couldn't understand why this was happening. There must be some mistake, he kept saying. He demanded he call his attorney. But the woman who served the court order told him that if he "opened his mouth one more time," unless it was to answer one of her questions, he was going to jail. He became cooperative in a hurry.

The marshalls seized boxes and boxes of black foam tubes. They seized piles of pink plastic caps and yellow plastic caps. They seized hundreds of assembled Thigh Magics, 22 to a box. Designs and drawings were confiscated, along with packaging and promotional materials. Breitinger could do nothing. He lit one cigarette after another and watched the marshalls load the product onto the truck.

I stood by and looked on. I could only imagine how he felt. On the other hand, I had little sympathy for him and looked forward to the hearing.

The next ten days flew by, and before I knew it, I was on the steps of the U.S. District Courthouse in Los Angeles, all because of a little thigh exerciser. I couldn't believe it. The federal courthouse in

L.A. resembles a mausoleum; it's one of those imposing white buildings that date from the 1920s or 1930s. Missing were the cast of characters you see in municipal court—the wife beaters, the drug dealers, the pimps, the muggers. In their place were pasty-looking men in gray suits. I couldn't tell the attorneys from the clients.

And Judge Hatter's courtroom was nothing like you see on *Perry Mason*. Thoroughly modern and renovated, it was cold and sterile, due in large part to a gigantic slab of green marble behind the bench that stretched from the floor to the ceiling. And there were no windows, either. It was like a big box. You felt cut off from the rest of the world.

I sat next to Ed, nervously tearing a paper cup and waiting for Hatter to arrive. While I tore up the cup several gorgeous young women filed into the courtroom.

"*Who* are *they?*" I asked Ed.

"Hatter's law clerks," he answered without lifting his eyes.

Law clerks? They looked like models. I leaned over and whispered, "I'll bet they use the ThighMaster."

Ed grinned. "If they do, we've won," he replied, and winked.

I should be so lucky. A week before the hearing, I'd asked Mike Clark to brief me on what to expect. Here's what he told me:

"First off," he said, "these guys will probably admit that they've copied ThighMaster's butterfly shape. And they'll shrug. Why? Because it's not a problem; it's not protectable, they'll say. Now, to claim protection under trade dress we'll have to prove that the shape is decorative, not utilitarian. Utilitarian means the shape is dictated by what the product's meant to do."

"Give me an example," I said.

"Okay, a shovel. The shape is utilitarian. It's the only shape that works to dig dirt. So it's not protectable by trade dress and would not be granted a design patent. However, it might get a utility patent if it was invented today instead of thousands of years ago. On the other hand, a zebra-striped shovel with a fur-covered handle might be protectable under design law. The additions are purely decorative."

"All rise," said the bailiff. Judge Hatter entered. He was a black man with gold wire-frame glasses. With his robes and white collar, he could have passed for a preacher—until he took his seat at the bench. There, surveying the courtroom, he looked like God on high.

Sure enough, their lawyer argued that the act of exercising the inner thighs dictated the butterfly shape of the Thigh Magic. He claimed that, to achieve firmer thigh muscles, one had to squeeze something shaped like the ThighMaster. You needed handles because you needed to press against something and the handles had to be covered in foam for comfort. It was a matter of utility, not aesthetics—which meant, he said, that Ovation wasn't entitled to trade-dress protection. Further, since Ovation hadn't applied for a utility patent, the utilitarian design of the ThighMaster was up for grabs. Case closed.

But Ed was no slouch, either. He argued forcefully that, no, you *could* firm up your inner thigh muscles without using an exercise device shaped like the ThighMaster. Why, look at the old V-Bar, designed by Anne-Marie Bennstrom, he said, waving the metal V in the air. It looked as much like the ThighMaster as a Model T looks like a Taurus. And what about this product, he said, holding up a large rubber ball that you stuck between your knees and squeezed to achieve shapely hips and thighs. For good measure, Ed submitted photos of other exercise devices—a boomerang-shaped thing and a tension coil with wooden handles on either end, and so on. And as far as proving the product is recognizable to the public, well, just watch the videotapes of Leno and Letterman cracking jokes. Was there anyone in America who *didn't* know what the ThighMaster looked like?

Judge Hatter sat with his hands clasped under his chin. I could see the fluorescent ceiling lights bouncing off his gold wedding band. He swiveled in his chair, asked some questions, but otherwise, sat motionless and silent. When the hearing was over, all I could think about was that the fate of the company was in his hands. How this federal judge ruled would determine Ovation's future. My future.

When the order came out, Hatter found that Ovation had a valid, protected trade dress that had been infringed. I was elated. It was a tremendous high.

A few days later, the Valley Boys, as Ed and Mike and I had grown fond of calling them, moved to settle. We agreed. We allowed them to sell off their inventory, but they had to pay us a royalty. They couldn't take any profits. And they couldn't make or sell any more Thigh Magics. That was the deal.

And what became of them? Well, believe it or not, MacGregor is now Bill Heichert's partner (yes, the same Bill Heichert who tipped me off to the Thigh Magic knock-offs to begin with). Breitinger even worked for them for a while. This is how the game is played in the infomercial industry.

Why? Well, for one thing, it's pointless to hold a grudge. The life cycle of an infomercial campaign can be short. People who sue each other on Monday reach a settlement on Tuesday and enter into negotiations for another product on Wednesday. Litigation is part of doing business. Goes with the territory. In fact, suits are filed with settlement in mind. How so? Well, with a simple letter and a phone call you can make ten times what you spend for the attorney to file the suit. This should tell you something else about this business: Intellectual property attorneys are as indispensible as the remote control.

This wouldn't be the last time we went to court to protect the ThighMaster. The Valley Boys were a threat to its prosperity, but there was a greater danger lurking in the shadows.

The day the raids took place, I was on top of the world. I couldn't believe how easy it had been to get these guys. Randee and I had just returned home from a celebratory dinner at Musso & Frank's, on Hollywood Boulevard, when the telephone rang. It was my buddy Jim McNamara.

"I'm faxing you something from the *Daily News*," he said. The *News* is the San Fernando Valley's daily paper. Jim lived in the Valley. "You're not gonna like it, Peter."

I hung up and ran downstairs to my office. It was a full-page ad, advertising a product that looked identical to the ThighMaster for $9.95. The ad was cleverly worded. It drew sharp distinctions between the advertised product and our own, turning them into sales points. The copy said, in effect, "Why pay a star a royalty on an exerciser when you can buy ours for half the price?" There was a footnote, too, acknowledging our trademark and company name.

I called Ed Glynn and faxed it to him at home. He guessed that the copywriter was working hand-in-glove with an attorney or maybe was an attorney himself. Ed and I agreed to talk in the morning.

The ad was bad enough. But the rumors I'd been hearing about ships with 30,000 units of knock-off product just off the Jersey shore made me more uneasy. Things were beginning to unravel. Fast. How would I stop it? *Could* I stop it?

The next day, I got another phone call. It was from Eddie Mishan. Eddie's company, Emson, is based in New York City. An import/export/manufacturing business, it was started in 1946 by his father, Ike. Eddie, I knew, was one of the premier knock-off artists in the direct-response business. (Eddie would deny this, of course, and, indeed, he seems intent on reform. His most recent hit, BaconWave, was an original.) At the time he called me, Artmark-Chicago was suing him for knocking off Artmark's line of crystal bells and their distinctive packaging. (In August 1992, Artmark would be awarded damages in excess of $1 million against Eddie.) More relevant to me, however, he was still engaged in a legal dispute with A. J. Khubani over a cat-and-mouse watch he'd knocked off. (I'll tell you the story in a minute.)

"You're the guy who's got the ThighMaster, right?" said Eddie in a heavy New York accent. "Have you seen the ad in the *Daily News?*" Yeah, I told him, wondering what the hell he was calling me about. "You know who's behind the ad, don't you? Khubani. A. J. Khubani. He's trying to get you to sue him. He's gonna call you and he's gonna push your buttons, try to get you to call him a jerk and threaten to sue him, so that he can seek a declaratory judgment. Then, of course, you'll want to cut a deal with him to avoid the expense of litigation. Be careful what you say to him, pal. Don't give him the satisfaction. The guy's a piece of work."

Click.

I was more than familiar with A. J. Khubani. He was a legend in his own time, a knock-off artist par excellence. He had a reputation in the infomerial business as someone who'd kill your direct-response campaign by selling his copies to the retailers, who'd sell them for half the price. Your phones stopped ringing.

A. J. was born in New Jersey, but his parents were from India. He worked for his father's importing company for less than a year before starting his own company in 1983 with $20,000 in savings. He was 23. By 1986, he made a net profit of $3 million from $11 million in sales. It was a mail-order business, print ads only.

In 1987, he discovered infomercials. He did a joint venture with a guy who knew the business, and they hawked an ultrasonic flea collar. A. J. had seen the product selling on the new Home Shopping Network and just went ahead and made his own. But there was a patent on the product, and the fellow who held the patent came after him.

It was his first taste of patent law. He stopped selling the flea collar, but he didn't stop knocking people off. He just boned up on intellectual property law.

A. J. knocked off the trendy Blue Blocker sunglasses, which sold for $59.95. Targeting the masses, he produced Amber Vision sunglasses for $10. He sold about 2 million pieces, a million off TV alone. He got them into Herman's sporting goods stores, too. They sold out. From there on, there was no stopping him. By 1990, he was doing $60 million in sales.

That was the same year that A. J. and Eddie Mishan locked horns in court, to the amusement of the rest of industry. A. J. claimed that Eddie's Playful Kitty Wrist Watch was a knock-off of his own Cat and Mouse Watch, which had grossed $20 million in sales. Unbelievable as it seems, A. J. actually owned the two copyrights for the product, and so he obtained a preliminary injunction.

The face on A. J.'s watch showed a long-haired gray tabby with a rotating black mouse as the second hand. The face on Eddie's watch also showed a gray tabby and a black mouse acting as the second hand. Eddie's near-slavish reproduction, not to mention his use of a red banner reading "AS NATIONALLY ADVERTISED" when he was doing no advertising of any kind, led the federal judge in the case to stop Eddie's sale (at half price) of his Playful Kitty watches pending a trial, which could take a year or two.

Poor Eddie. He was stuck with a warehouse full of cat-and-mouse watches that he couldn't ship. Worse, the watches had batteries that were slowly going dead. It was going to be cheaper to throw them away than replace the batteries. By the time a trial was concluded, nobody would want the watches anyway. The fad would be over. No wonder he hated A. J.

The day after we defeated the Valley Boys in Judge Hatter's courtroom, there was a telephone message to call Keith Mirchandani at A. J.'s company. With some trepidation, I returned the call. Keith immediately got A. J. on the phone. Just as Eddie predicted, A. J. baited me. "Are you going to sue me?" he said. I replied calmly that I didn't know, but we were defending our rights very aggressively. "I know," he said. "I had lawyers in the courtroom yesterday." He did? I felt a sense of forboding.

He proceeded to lay things out for me. We could work together or we could fight it out in court, which could cost us each about $200,000 in legal fees. And, on top of that, if I should try to seize his product, I'd have to put up a $5 million bond, a much bigger outlay than was required in the Valley Boys case because A. J. had so much more product. What he wanted was to market a lower-priced version of the ThighMaster, and he was prepared to give me a royalty.

More legal fees, a $5 million bond—this could be a serious problem for a tiny company with all its assets tied up in inventory and media commitments. On the other hand, a partner with strong retail distribution paying us fat royalties might work. Feeling ambivalent, I told him I was interested in talking with him. He offered to fly to L.A. immediately to pursue our discussions. We set a date.

We met at the Hamlet Gardens restaurant in Westwood, within walking distance of my office. I was about five minutes late, so when I got there, he was already seated in a corner booth. He was younger than I expected and dressed nattily in a loose jacket. I'd already worked out the deal I wanted to strike with him. If I made a deal at all, I wanted to keep the knock-off product off the market as long as possible, at least until the third quarter of '92, so I'd have a clear field for nine months. On top of that, I wanted to get paid $3 a unit and I wanted him to commit to a quality product.

A.J. had a counterproposal. He wanted to give me a dollar a unit. And he stressed the importance of making money while the money could be made. Other competitors would jump into the market by the fourth quarter, he said, and if he wasn't out there, he'd lose out completely. He wanted to put his cheaper knock-off out right away. I also met stiff resistance to my request that he call the product something other than Thigh-this or Thigh-that. He said it had to be called Thigh-something.

The food came. Over lunch, he described his activities, including his ongoing lawsuit with Eddie Mishan. He said he knew he had a bad reputation but that he didn't consider himself a knock-off king. What he did was compete. He explained that his company, Telebrands, was emerging as a distributor to retail, that he was constantly looking for products to take retail. Whenever he saw an infomercial hit, he came up with a competing product. (Today, he focuses on developing originals.) The infomercial companies were mostly start-ups; they were still figuring out the mail-order business. They weren't thinking about the next move. Why shouldn't he beat them to the punch? He wasn't doing anything illegal. And besides, the consumers won. Instead of paying $30 for product sold through television, they could pay $20 for a similar item at Wal-Mart. "The consumer always wins in a competitive environment," he said. Isn't that what he'd learned in college? Wasn't that the American Way?

What he left out was that none of these knock-off products would get into stores or move off the shelves without the product development and ad campaign paid for by the other guy. Of course, while A. J. saved here, he spent more on legal fees.

Lunch was over, and there were still two major issues on the table: price and timing. After the check was paid, just as we were about to get up, I turned to A. J. and said, okay, let's make a deal. You can bring your product into the marketplace on February 28th and the price is three dollars. January 1st and one dollar, he shot back. I responded February 1st, two dollars, and we shook hands. We agreed to talk in a day or two to get the paperwork going.

While I paid the check, I asked him what A. J. stood for. "Ajit," he said. "It means 'unconquerable' in Hindi."

I walked back to the office feeling I'd made the best of a bad situation. But the deal collapsed almost immediately. When I called A. J., he was never in and my calls were not returned. I started to grow suspicious. Then I heard reports that he'd bought air time on TV for his product, a violation of our agreement. When I finally got hold of A. J. on the phone, I told him that if he wasn't going to deal with me in an honest and straightforward fashion, that I couldn't see how we could do business together. He started to complain about the deal, that he wasn't able to bring the product to market soon enough and that I was charging him too much. We left it on that note. The deal was obviously off. I *never* threatened to sue him.

The following morning we were served with a summons. A. J., having claimed that I threatened to sue him, demanded a declaratory judgment in federal district court in New Jersey.

It was a surprise attack on our company that sent me reeling. Judging by the date of the sworn affidavits included in the summons, I figured A. J. left Los Angeles intending to sue me, possibly even *came* to town intending to sue me and had used our negotiations as a way of stalling me so I wouldn't sue him first, which would have dragged him into court in Los Angeles.

He was five moves ahead of me on the chessboard. Scary.

His legal maneuver was to seek a judicial opinion on whether or not our trade dress was valid; his business aim was to clear the path of road blocks and come after us. Because he had an operation in New Jersey, he could take advantage of the third circuit, which had a tough standard for trade-dress protection—bad for us, good for him.

I talked to Ed Glynn, who told me Jim Myers was free now and that he would be my counsel for this round. I talked with Jim over the phone, and, when the court date approached, we met for dinner at the airport Marriott in Newark.

• • •

After we talked for a while, it struck me as ironic that Jim, a Harvard-trained lawyer, a man who'd been lead trial counsel in a wide variety of patent infringement litigation for major international, Fortune 500, and high technology companies, was now applying his considerable intellectual candlepower to defending a thigh exerciser. This was not unusual for him.

As the infomercial industry had grown, so had the need for attorneys. The more entrepreneurs pushed the legal boundaries—the more they skirted the edges of patent law—the more they landed in court. Never mind that the products were comparatively slight, inconsequential, sometimes humorous; Millions of dollars were on the table. And where there's a fortune at stake, there are lawyers. Good ones. Venable had discovered a lucrative niche. Infomercial law now represents a major piece of business for the firm.

Although he'd never tangled with A. J. in court, Jim knew his reputation and what kind of moves we could expect.

"Most people look at court as a way to resolve a conflict. Some people in this industry look at going to court as a tactic in a negotiation. It's a way to put pressure on the other side," said Jim. What he was telling me was that, while the average guy looks at going to court with dread, A. J. treated the courtroom as an extension of his boardroom.

The hearing was set for two weeks from the day that the papers were served. Two judgments would be issued: (1) on A. J.'s request that any suit against him be adjudicated in the third circuit and (2) on our simultaneous suit against him to enjoin or prevent him from selling his product until we could go to trial on trade-dress infringement.

Jim and I were highly optimistic. First of all, we had the California case decided in our favor. Second, A. J.'s product, Thigh Shaper, was even more of a knock-off than Thigh Magic. Third, we had, of course, all the usual arguments we'd used against Thigh Magic, including photographs of other thigh-firming products. How could we lose?

Newark, New Jersey is the purest definition of urban decay. Despite signs welcoming visitors to "America's Renaissance City," it has, by all appearances, been written off by the nation, let alone the people in the state. There are liquor stores, lottery-ticket vendors, laundromats, photo-ID places, quickie marts, and not much else. Except court buildings. In this last respect, downtown Newark looks like one big WPA project.

The interior of the federal courthouse stands in stark contrast to the blight beyond its walls. It is splendid. The corridor outside the courtroom of Judge John W. Bissell, the judge who would hear our case, was like the hallway of an Italian palazzo. There were glistening marble floors and grand Corinthian columns. Voices echoed loudly, as in some vast and lonely palace.

Judge Bissell's courtroom was no less impressive. Here was sobriety and tradition as one only finds on the East Coast. Suspended from the ceiling, which was decorated with gold leaf, were pewter and copper chandeliers. The windows, which were grand, were framed in red velvet drapes. The walls, wood-paneled, of course. *This* is a courtroom, I said to myself.

Bissell, I learned from Jim, was a family man; an eastern Republican who didn't suffer fools gladly. Analytical. Direct. There is probably no position in America closer to having dictatorial powers than being a federal district court judge, Jim reminded me. Wielding that much power, he added, could engender vastly different attitudes on the part of those on the bench.

The judge was late for the 9 A.M. hearing, which gave me a chance to say hello to A. J., who was sitting on a marble bench outside the courtroom with his two attorneys. He expressed surprise that I'd turned up for the hearing, and I said that I wasn't going to miss the fireworks for anything. I was so sure we were going to win that I anticipated this being a pleasant experience and felt little of the nervousness that I had felt at the Los Angeles hearing.

At 10 A.M., Judge Bissell arrived. To our great surprise, he was carrying an old V-Bar. He apologized for being late, then proceeded to explain the V-Bar. He said he was discussing the case with his wife and daughter at breakfast when his daughter said, "Dad, I've got one of those. I picked it up at a garage sale for $2." She got it for him, and he brought it to the courtroom.

This was great. It was almost as though the judge walked in carrying an exhibit for the defense. We needed to prove that a thigh exerciser did not have to have the butterfly shape of the Thigh-Master. The V-Bar made the point. The judge laid down the questions he wanted answered, most of them quite technical and aimed at getting the attorneys to present their sides of the argument of whether or not the design of the ThighMaster was dictated by function or aesthetics.

Thomas Carulli, A. J.'s lead attorney, was the first to address the court. He began by saying that it was very clear from Ovation's advertising that the ThighMaster shape was functional—"They tell the consumer a doctor invented this, spent years creating it, it's effective for this muscle group. It's designed specifically for this muscle group," and so forth. He tried to poke a hole through our argument that the product was widely recognizable by claiming that Suzanne Somers, not the shape or color of the ThighMaster, was emphasized in our ads. Hence, it was she, and not the product, who was recognizable. But his main point was that there was no protectable aesthetic design here. He cited no case law and he never really addressed the judge's technical questions.

Now it was Jim's turn. In contrast, he was very precise in his responses to the judge's questions, and he cited plenty of cases to support our contention that there were many ways to make a thigh exerciser. He argued that the significance of the V-Bar was that it was indisputable evidence that there were different ways of accomplishing the same exercise. What the folks at Ovation had done, he said, was take an ugly device and give it the attractive butterfly shape to make it saleable. He concluded that the design of our product was ornamental.

Way to go, Jim.

But now the judge was asking what would happen if Telebrands was let into the marketplace. He wanted to know who would suffer the greatest economic harm—us if they came in, or them if they were kept out. I didn't like it. When the hearing was over, I felt a lot less confident than before it began.

There was a recess until 3 P.M., when Judge Bissell delivered his opinion. First, he acknowledged that the issuance of a design patent for the ThighMaster from the Patent Office was very likely. Second, he said the court was aware that the defendent (Ovation) had obtained a preliminary injunction in California securing trade-dress protection.

But, he also noted, that the current plaintiff (Telebrands) was not a party to *that* action, that it was a decision issuing out of the ninth circuit rather than the third circuit. "Accordingly, it's not a decision that's binding upon this court, although to be sure, it's entitled to some measure of deference." So much for Judge Hatter's opinion.

I cast a worried glance at Jim.

The judge went on to quote from my affidavit, and he turned my testimony against me: "Josh Reynolds," he read, "manager of V-Partners, an inventor and exercise specialist, further reengineered the ThighMaster for over two years. . . ." Reengineered. That one word hurt us. If only I'd chosen my words more carefully. Reengineered implied a functional alteration, not an aesthetic one.

The judge ruled in favor of A. J. He was free to manufacture and sell his product unfettered. We would have another chance to stop him when the patent was granted but that was many, many months away.

I was stunned.

Next thing I knew, Jim was talking with the other attorneys on our side. They were making noise about it being a reversible decision, the court of appeals would be sympathetic, and so on and so forth, discussing all the options in a lawyerly fashion. Meanwhile, I was sitting there thinking about shrinking revenues and high legal bills.

Across the room, A. J., all smiles, was hugging his attorneys and shaking their hands. He was free to sell his product and siphon off my sales. My phones would go dead.

A. J. strode out of the courtroom with his contingent. I hung my head. Stared at the floor. My lawyers continued to drone on about the appeals process for another half hour. I barely listened.

Suddenly A. J. reappeared in the door. I was surprised. I thought he'd left the building. He said he wanted to talk to me in private. We walked out into the corridor and started pacing. It was early evening, the courthouse was deserted, and our footsteps echoed off the marble floor. I congratulated him on his victory, and he said it felt good. But he had an offer for me. He wanted to settle.

Huh? My mind raced. Settle? He won. Why did he want to settle? He explained the situation. Tomorrow the judge was going to make his opinion public, and the whole world would know that the ThighMaster was not protected. So every knock-off guy in the business would be on the phone to Taiwan, putting in their orders. A. J. wanted to restrict the market to him and me. The way to accomplish that was to prevent the opinion from being published by reaching a settlement right away. He made me a rock-bottom offer, fifty cents for every unit he sold.

The man was unbelievable!

It was getting late, and the attorneys on his side were expressing some concerns about walking to their cars in downtown Newark after dark. We agreed to meet in the morning to discuss licensing the rights. It was decided that the pow-wow would take place at Khubani's attorneys' offices, 30 Rockefeller Plaza in New York.

The next day, before we began the negotiations, Jim insisted on having a confidentiality agreement signed that guaranteed that whatever we said and discussed would not leave the room and would not be used as part of any further proceedings. As it turned out, this document played an important part in the way this story concludes.

The negotiations ran from 11 A.M. to around 5 P.M. in the afternoon. Most of the time it was just me and A. J., eyeball to eyeball. Occasionally, the attorneys popped in. When it was over, there were still some major points that hadn't been discussed in any detail, such as the amount of liquidated damages. It also wasn't clear whether we were truly licensing him the trade dress or only agreeing not to sue him if he infringed on it. His attorneys said they would draft an agreement and that we would have it by Friday, the day after tomorrow.

The plane ride home was awful. No, there wasn't a hint of turbulence. I just felt lousy. I was so depressed. The good face I'd put on the deal started melting like wax. All the rationalization in the world couldn't hide the fact that I didn't want to be in business with A. J.

Several things happened over the next few days to confirm I'd made a mistake in teaming up with him. First, we received no contract from his attorneys on Friday as promised. The last time A. J. had missed his deadline, he had been stalling to give himself time to sue me. Second, Bill Heichert called and told me he was getting word back from the field that A. J. was informing the trade that he had a license to sell our product—this was in violation of the confidentiality agreement. Third, we heard rumors that A. J. was placing television advertising, another violation. All this and only three days after shaking hands.

The deal was dead. I knew it. He didn't. Perhaps I could use that to my advantage.

It was time to switch to the offensive.

I telephoned Jim Myers. I had an idea. What if we put out a letter, by fax, to the trade, explaining that A. J. did not have a license to sell the ThighMaster. This would put him in a very bad fix. Many stores that already had product would ship it back, and others would refuse to place orders because they did not want to be stuck with product that could be seized by marshalls. Ironically, the idea of warning the retailers had come to me as a result of something A. J. had said during our lunch at Hamlet Gardens in Westwood. In his dispute with Eddie Mishan over the cat-and-mouse watch, he sent a warning out about Eddie's knock-offs. The retailers sent back the watches. More dead mice in the warehouse.

We faxed about one hundred twenty letters. We rented an extra fax machine so that we could run two of them at once. This way, if word got back to A. J. that it was happening, we'd be through most of the work before he could take any action to stop us. We made it clear in the letter that we intended to appeal Judge Bissell's opinion as well. We got the faxes out in about an hour and a half.

A. J. screamed. Stores were calling left and right to cancel their Thigh Shaper orders. He was outraged. Couldn't believe it. Why had I not tried to work out the problems with him?

I felt pretty good after that phone call. I'd undermined his credibility in the marketplace regarding his right to sell Thigh Shapers.

I'd kept him out of the field for a significant period of time. And I still had the possibility of going after him, tooth and fang as soon as my patent was issued.

I slept like a baby that night.

As Jim predicted, Telebrands filed a motion to enforce a settlement. A. J. had God-knows-how-much product on its way from the Far East. He needed a decision. I had a lot at stake, too. If the settlement was enforced, I would be the one to lose his credibility.

I flew back east.

The thrust of Jim's argument before Judge Bissell was that the *purported* settlement should not be enforced because significant issues had not been fully negotiated, that discussions had not ripened into an enforceable agreement.

A. J.'s attorney made a strong case that we were trying to weasel out of the agreement. (He didn't use those words, but that was the impression he left.) He said Ovation had a settlement it didn't want implemented. And the breaches we were claiming? Nothing much. A letter was late, some rumors of TV ads. Big deal.

Things didn't look too good. Again.

So, Jim took a calculated risk. He put me on the stand. With land-mine-dodging precision, he pursued a line of questioning that allowed me to recount the difficulties I'd had with A. J.

An unflattering portrait emerged.

I recounted how he'd lied that I'd threatened to sue him, which landed me in court to begin with; how he'd flown to Los Angeles to discuss licensing the trade dress rights to our product only to turn around and serve me papers. I told the Court how astounded I was that he'd broken the confidentiality agreement he signed at his attorney's offices in New York.

Time and again, he proved himself untrustworthy.

My testimony helped convince the judge that this marriage shouldn't take place. The motion to enforce the settlement was denied. The Judge wrote in his opinion that the "plaintiff in fact has [himself] to blame for the demise of the settlement negotiations." There was the unexplainable delay in getting the contract to us on Friday, and, secondly, "by jumping the gun with potential distributors by disclosing the oral discussions prematurely to them, the plaintiff really cooked its own goose."

A.J.'s Thigh Shaper campaign limped along. Retailers were still reluctant to stock his product after my fax blitz. If he was going to make another big push into the market, it would have to be after our patent was published, and he challenged it. Presuming he was successful.

When I got notice of the publication, I jumped the gun on him. We immediately moved for a preliminary injunction, seeking to prevent A.J. from making and selling his Thigh Shapers. The key would be to convince the judge (yep, Bissell) that the standard for a design patent was different than for trade dress.

It was a tall order for Jim. He'd have to get the judge to reverse his earlier opinion. To admit he'd been wrong when he'd claimed the ThighMaster's distinctive shape was dictated by functional rather than decorative considerations. Not a likely scenario. Unless, of course, there was a way to save face (not to mention, a very good legal reason for why he should reach such a conclusion).

Jim came up with a creative strategy. He decided to play into the preconceptions that he supposed existed on the part of this conservative, East-Coast-Republican judge. Jim argued that the bunch of people who created the ThighMaster couldn't engineer their way out of a paper bag, that they couldn't recognize a functional design if they fell over one. How so? Because they were flakes. After the hearing, I flew home, crossing my fingers that Jim's gamble paid off.

Two weeks later Jim was back in the courtroom to hear Judge Bissell's decision. I remained in California. On Jim's way into the courthouse, A. J. stopped him. He made the same low-ball offer he'd made before: fifty cents a unit and we tell the judge we have a deal. If I didn't take his offer, he told Jim, I'd lose everything. He shrugged, like why be stupid?

Jim gave me a call. What did I want to do? I swallowed hard. "Tell him, 'No deal.' "

148

Thirty minutes later Jim phoned back. With a flair for the dramatic, Jim told me how his strategy had worked. The judge described the people who developed the product as an eclectic group of Californians, including a television producer, a psychic advisor, the owner of a health spa, and an entrepreneur with a bachelor's degree in psychology. Not an engineer among them. Better, he had quoted directly from Josh Reynold's deposition, in which Josh described how he saw the ThighMaster in a meditative state at two in the morning. What came to him was a primal, archetypal design, the shape of a butterfly or the infinity symbol, so that the design of the ThighMaster was based in Jungian psychology and the force of certain symbols on the psyche.

I was laughing so hard I was crying. Jim had called it right. As a result, A. J. was dead in the water. Barred from the marketplace. We'd won.

"Great job, buddy. A million thanks."

"Don't thank me," said Jim. "Thank Carl Jung."

CHAPTER · 7

$100,000,000

I could hardly believe it. The ThighMaster was going retail.

I'd gone through so much to get here. I'd convinced Pippa that using direct-response strategies to drive retail sales was a bankable idea. I'd found a quality product, something that looked good and also felt good in your hands. I'd maneuvered Suzanne into a leotard, knowing her sexy image on a box would make Thigh-Master easy to spot on store shelves. I'd chosen a price of $19.95 instead of $29.95 so that I could play the ad more widely and thus support my retail sales. All along the line, decisions were made with one goal in mind: a retail launch.

The direct-response campaign was just a means to an end. If all I accomplished was just a successful TV campaign, I think I'd have left the business feeling like a failure. Frankly, I didn't want to be lumped together with hucksters selling doo-dads and gizmos out of a PO box. Sure, I was borrowing their strategies—theirs was the only kind of TV campaign I could afford! But I saw myself as a mainstream manufacturer, selling products where most people buy them—in stores.

And, as far as direct response goes, I was breaking the rules. Traditionally, direct-response advertisers didn't take chances with their infomercial revenues. They let the ad campaign run its course until saturation drove the cost per order into unprofitable territory, until the phones had just about stopped ringing. *Then* they put the product into retail. It was almost an afterthought.

Which brings me to Victor Grillo.

Victor distributed a wide variety of products to retail, many of them infomercial hits. His company, Direct To Retail, was based outside of Boston. He'd been calling me because he wanted to beat his competitors to the retail rights for the ThighMaster. Though he and A. J. were after the same thing—the chance to take ThighMaster retail—their tactics were different. Victor was a gentleman. He didn't try to intimidate me into handing him the retailing rights. He called me up, introduced himself, and made his intentions known.

But, boy, was he persistent. He wouldn't take no for an answer. (Now I know how Connie Halperin felt when I hounded her for a date in high school.)

Victor made his final offer: a million-dollar guaranteed royalty payment. Would I sign? I talked to Pippa and Joe. We all said no. Well, he sighed, that was the best he could do. He wished me luck and hung up.

I'm sure he thought I was crazy, but I'd never had any doubt about taking ThighMaster retail *myself.* I'd planned to do so from the start. I wanted to create a company with real value, with the ability to service major accounts and manufacture products because, well, I hoped to take the company public.

I didn't need Victor. Or A. J.

Another thing: My business plan called for putting the product into stores when the campaign was in full swing, when we were spending money each week on media, when everyone was talking about the product and the stores were clamoring for it—*not one year later when the excitement was over.* This was a radical approach.

Yet, as much as I'd believed in the plan six months ago, I found myself wavering. Success felt good, *real* good. I hadn't expected that. Going retail *now,* at the height of the media campaign, would be like leaving a swell party to go across town and crash another you weren't so sure about. Here, there was wine, women, and song. At the other party—who knows? Maybe three lonely guys and a bag of chips.

It was inevitable that the minute the ThighMaster became available in stores, some people would put off buying it on TV. With very thin margins on a large volume, a slight increase in the CPO would make the campaign unprofitable.

The question was, was there enough pent-up demand in the retail market to make up for lost direct-response sales? If so, I could keep the campaign on the air and use it to drive my retail sales.

Before I committed to a retail launch *now,* just when the campaign was smokin', I decided to do some market research. We'd already been selling ThighMasters at state and county fairs and at the Orange County Swap Meet. The Swap Meet is a kind of open-air mall. You can buy anything there, from a grand piano to kitchen cabinets to lawn and garden tools—all of it new. ("Swap Meet" is a total misnomer.) Swaps are popular out here because everything's in one place. They save you a lot of travel time.

I chose the Orange County Swap Meet because it was the closest thing to a retail environment. Bill Heichert had done a nice job with the booth. He had balloons and bunting and blue and red folding chairs. He placed a ThighMaster on each chair to encourage people to sit down and try our product. Kind of like a shoe store. I had a clipboard in my hand and Holly with me, in a backpack.

I approached the people who bought a ThighMaster and asked them a couple of questions: Where had they heard of the Thigh-

Master? If they had seen the ad on television, why hadn't they bought one? Had they ever bought *anything* off television?

Virtually everyone who'd bought a ThighMaster at the Swap Meet had seen the ad on TV, but there was always some excuse for not buying it off the tube: they didn't have time, or they were planning to but didn't get around to it; they didn't catch the telephone number when they saw the ad, or they wanted to talk to their spouse about buying it, so on and so on. What it amounted to was they bought it when they saw it in person. They didn't hesitate.

This is what I learned at the Swap Meet: One out of five people who want to buy your product will buy it off television; the other four will wait until it's in the stores, and, if it never gets there, they'll never buy it.

We were selling thousands and thousands of ThighMasters on television, and yet there were *four times* as many waiting to be sold in stores. I started feeling more confident about going retail when the direct-response campaign was going full blast.

I hung back a while and just watched people buy.

The ThighMasters were sitting on their chairs, and the women—they were mostly women—just walked right up to them like they were meeting an old friend. They'd pick one up, sit down in the chair, put it between their knees, and start squeezing. Others just got in line—no need for a test squeeze. It was exciting, a bit like watching your kid on her first day of kindergarten. I was so *proud.*

After the Swap Meet, I started thinking about packaging. An appealing package isn't important in direct response; a sturdy brown box will do. Your customers have already made their buying decision while watching your ad on television. Retail is different. The package needs to be eye-catching, it needs to remind people of the ad, of course, and the copy has to sell the product. The customer will make her decision standing in an aisle, under bright lights, surrounded by other shoppers. She may be tired or in a hurry. The package must connect. Our VP marketing Carol Land and freelance designer Phil Groves met the challenge of discount-store merchandising, where boxes are stacked any which way: Suzanne beckoned from every side of the box and on the ends, too. You couldn't miss her.

At the same time, I started putting together a national sales force. What happened was, a sales rep contacted me because buyers were calling him looking for the ThighMaster. (This is what happens when you have a hit product on television. People see your ad on TV and ask for the product in stores. The sales clerks tell the managers that people are asking, so the managers tell the buyers. Then, the buyers start looking for reps who can sell them the product.) I told him we hadn't gone retail yet but that I was looking to hire a master rep to help me assemble a sales force. Did he know anyone who was good and could start immediately?

He mentioned Randy Akers.

Randy was an independent sales rep who lived in Reno, Nevada. He represented several lines of sporting goods, and sporting goods was the closest thing to my category. He was smart, aggressive, and eager to take the job. I hired him.

Randy and I divided the country into seven sales regions and hired a rep for each one. Some of these people were recommended by buyers at the major chains; some of them Randy knew. It was a relatively easy process; almost everyone we talked to had seen the ad on TV. They were already familiar with the product.

That done, we contracted with a factoring service. A factor buys your receivables at a discount and goes after the stores for the money. In other words, it functions like a collection agency. One of the biggest reasons people in direct response stay out of retail is the fear that the chains will screw them. Thirty days becomes sixty, sixty days becomes ninety—and still no check. Which leads to a major cash crunch for the manufacturer: He's bearing all the costs. Direct response, by comparison, is so simple; so easy. It's a cash business. The customers pay for the product before they get it! What could be more beautiful?

I agree. Direct response *is* beautiful. But going retail doesn't have to be a dicey proposition. If you use a factoring service, for a fairly modest fee, you remove the credit risk and shorten your cash-flow risk. No headaches, no hassles.

And there was a major advantage to having a boffo media campaign: Customers asked for the ThighMaster before it was in the stores. That made it easier for our sales reps. When they started knocking on doors, they got a warm reception from buyers.

The small chains called first, typically sporting goods outlets. Our West Coast rep called with an order from Copeland's in Southern California for about 2,000 ThighMasters. Then he called back with an order from Oshman's, out of Houston, for more than 10,000.

Next, our reps heard from the regional department stores. Venture, out of Missouri, wanted more than 10,000 units. Fred Meyer, a retailer in the Pacific Northwest, called in an order. Every week we heard from more stores. Bradlees. Shopko.

And then the stores started calling back. This was a turning point. The first order meant the buyer had heard about ThighMaster and was willing to take a flyer on it. But a second order, close on its heels, meant the product was flying off the shelf. We were seeing big orders with very little time in between. What's more, the third and fourth orders were as large as the first!

Fairly soon, we heard from the big boys. From Woolworth, Target, and Wal-Mart.

Nobody *plans* to go to Woolworth except when it's time to buy thread or goldfish food. But Woolworth has many inner-city locations, near bus depots, train terminals, and subway stations, so the chain gets a lot of drop-in traffic from commuters picking up last-minute items. It's a perfect outlet for a heavily advertized impulse item. Like a ThighMaster. Plus the stores are in old buildings; they've got windows. Windows help move impulse purchases. For these reasons, Woolworth was an excellent outlet for selling a television product. After a small initial test, Woolworth's opening order was for more than 15,000 units.

Next, we heard from Target, the third largest discount chain after Wal-Mart and Kmart. This Minneapolis-based chain is also the most upscale of the big discount operators. It wasn't long before our sales rep was phoning me, excited that Target had sold $1 million worth of ThighMasters in one week, a record.

Then we heard from Wal-Mart. Wal-Mart changed the rules of retailing with its compelling merchandising strategy, emphasizing everyday low pricing supported by state-of-the-art inventory control. In 1990, its revenues topped Sears and Kmart and made it the nation's largest retailer. It's every manufacturer's dream to get on the shelves of Wal-Mart. If you get there at all, it takes years—unless, of course, you get a boost from a direct-response advertising campaign. Wal-Mart gave us a big opening order.

As Christmas approached, a recurring vision danced in my head. I pictured truckloads of ThighMasters traveling the back roads and highways of America. Thousands and thousands of them arriving daily in big cities and small towns, where they joined the panoply of consumer goods on the shelves of Woolworth, Wal-Mart, and Target. Hundreds of thousands of ThighMasters fanning out across the nation, feeding this great capitalist culture of consumption of ours.

It took my breath away.

But success is a taskmaster. Within a few months we were hundreds of thousands of units behind in production. Although the Phoenix factory was moving at full tilt, we just couldn't make 'em fast enough. All of us at the office were putting in sixteen-to-eighteen-hour days. It was hell. But it was heaven.

Meanwhile, we waited to hear from Kmart.

ThighMaster was the perfect Kmart product, but for some reason Kmart wasn't calling. A lot of people who saw the ThighMaster ad on TV shopped at Kmart, yet they couldn't purchase it there. It was costing me money to reach those Kmart shoppers every time I ran the ad. And when they couldn't buy the product where they shopped, I was throwing that money down the drain. It was maddening.

One of the best rep firms we employed handled the Michigan and Illinois area. They had a Kmart specialist who essentially camped out at Kmart's headquarters in Detroit.

It didn't help. Despite the fact that we'd had so much attention and the other big chains had placed orders with us, the rep was continually rebuffed.

It was time to take matters into my own hands. I decided to pay Kmart a call.

I flew to Detroit and our rep took me to meet their buyer. I quoted Wal-Mart's and Target's and Woolworth's figures. I told him that he was missing the opportunity of a lifetime; this was the hottest product in America. What was holding him back?

I wore him down. A few weeks later I got a call from my rep.

The buyer had been burned by the Tummysizer.

The Tummysizer was a $19.95 stomach exercise belt that operated on the basis of isometric contraction of muscles. Kmart sold it for $17.95. The buyer confessed to my rep that he was sitting on thousands of these things. Nobody wanted 'em. The product had been launched the previous year by Fitness Quest, the Canton, Ohio-based company that introduced the Abdomenizer, another stomach-firming device, and the Easy Glider and Fit One ski simulators. Both had been huge retail hits. The Tummysizer, alas, was not.

The problem was that it was dumb. All it did was count the number of times you contracted your stomach muscles. You could sit on the couch and drink beer and eat peanuts and push your stomach in and out, and look down to see how many times you'd flexed you abdominal muscles. It even made a clicking noise, as if to make you think it was really doing something. Sound like a gimmick to you? Sounded like one to me.

Kmart's culture at the time looked unkindly on mistakes. To have to go out and sell these things to a liquidator or remainder house was out of the question. It would mean admitting you screwed up. Maybe get canned. So the buyer was stuck with the Tummysizers until they finally sold out, which could take a very long time. Meanwhile, he had no room for the ThighMaster.

There was only one thing to do. We offered to buy them. All of them.

I knew that he couldn't sell them to a liquidator, but he could sell them to us—and then we could turn around and sell them to a liquidator. It would be our little secret. That way, he'd save face and the ThighMaster would get shelf space in Kmart!

A wacky deal? You bet. But, hey, major-chain shelf space is valuable real estate. When you're dealing with Kmart, you're dealing with more than 2,000 stores. That's a big hunk of your potential retail market. Believe me, you'll do anything to get on those shelves, including buying your biggest competitor's worst product, and buying it eagerly! As it turned out, the ThighMaster became the fastest-selling sporting goods product in Kmart's history.

It was great getting the ThighMaster into the big chains. Woolworth, Target, Wal-Mart, and Kmart ultimately would account for more than 50 percent of our business.

We were home free.

Except for one little problem. Actually, a big problem.

We started getting reports that scattered Wal-Mart stores were deep-discounting the ThighMaster, to $14.95. Why would it do this? Because hot products sold at a deep discount generate traffic for Wal-Mart, whose customers rarely leave the store without a full basket. Not true for the small owner-operated stores, the independent sporting goods stores and so forth. They can't compete with a loss-leader price. This meant they'd probably stop carrying our product. That could kill my campaign.

I started getting irate calls from Target, too. Their managers were locked into a uniform discounted price of $17.95. Stop 'em, they cried. Cut 'em off.

But it wasn't that simple. The law is strict on this subject. (Don't take my word for it. Talk to your own attorney.) You have to be very careful about what you say and do. A manufacturer cannot negotiate pricing with a retailer, although you may state your pricing policy. You can say, "We will not sell our product to any merchant who sells it for less than the suggested retail price." You can say that till the cows come home. But the minute you say, "*And unless you stop,*" you've broken the law. You've entered into a negotiation. That's called price-fixing.

I consulted with my attorney, read the legal opinion he gave me on the subject, and booked a trip to Bentonville, Arkansas. I called my regional sales rep and told him to meet me there.

Getting to Bentonville was an ordeal. I flew into Nashville, then got on a puddle jumper to Fayetteville, a town of 37,000 and the home of the University of Arkansas Razorbacks. Its other claim to fame is that President Clinton taught at the university. The flight to Fayetteville had maybe twenty-five people on it, all of them, I suspected, vendors headed to Wal-Mart's "home office," as the company so quaintly refers to its corporate headquarters. After the seat belt instructions, I half expected the flight attendant to do the Wal-Mart cheer ("Give me a W! Give me an A! Give me an L! Give me a squiggly . . .").

On the ground, I rented a car and drove the 30 miles to Bentonville. By the time I got there, I was exhausted, irritable, starving. I stayed at this terrible Best Western hotel, and then, in the morning, drove to Wal-Mart's offices outside of town with greasy eggs and grits laying on my stomach.

Wal-Mart's home office is like the Pentagon: an impregnable fortress. It dawned on me that, of the 11,000 people who live in Bentonville, almost half probably work in this one, enormous building. Across the street is a Wal-Mart super-store. (Not a job you want to have, being the manager of the Wal-Mart across the street from the corporate headquarters.)

It was clear that Sam Walton's everyday-low-pricing philosophy had been applied to the lobby's furnishings. There were linoleum tiles, blue plastic chairs, and row of pay telephones. When we arrived, a young woman in white pumps led us from the lobby to what she referred to as "the visitor's room." I saw that it was one of maybe ten cubicles off the lobby. Little more than a holding pen. There was a formica desk with a chair behind it, and, in front of the desk, another chair. I sat down. Bobby, my sales rep, remained standing. I noticed a camera in a corner of the ceiling. Bobby made a joke about the room being bugged. I laughed nervously.

At other stores, you got invited into the buyer's office, where you were offered a cup of coffee, sometimes a doughnut. There were usually pictures of the kids on the desk. There was always a bit of small talk before you got down to business. Here, the sterile, high-security environment suggested small talk was unlikely. Coffee was clearly out of the question.

The buyer walked in with another, taller, man who had short hair, almost a crew cut, and a military bearing. He was the buyer's supervisor. Both men were in shirtsleeves. The supervisor sat in the chair behind the desk. The buyer stood next to him. The supervisor leaned forward and addressed me:

"I don't like doin' things behind someone's back," he said in a dripping drawl. "So, I'm gonna be real up-front about this. We like Bobby, we think he's an awful nice fella, but don't you *ever* bring him back here."

I looked at Bobby. Bobby looked at me.

What I didn't realize was that Wal-Mart was pressuring all its vendors to dump their Wal-Mart reps. The company claimed that because it was placing more and more orders electronically, it didn't need them and wanted to avoid paying their commissions. Wherever possible, Wal-Mart continues to deal directly with manufacturers.

"Listen, Bieler, you're out of your depth," he said flatly. Then he proceeded to tell me I was breaking the law by even coming to talk with them. (I wasn't. He was just trying to intimidate me.) "You're a vendor," he said. "Leave retailing to the pros," he said.

Shaken but not about to roll over, I told him he was mistaken, that I knew *precisely* what I was doing. That I had no *intention* of negotiating price, if that's what he was implying. I simply wanted to make something clear. (Here, he grinned.) Choosing my words carefully, I told him that we retained the right to stop selling to anybody who broke our pricing policy. I stood up, we shook hands, and Bobby followed me out the door.

Wal-Mart never toed the line 100 percent, but they curtailed their deep discounting substantially. So I guess the trip was worth it.

And the relationship continued to be a good one—Wal-Mart was our biggest account—although it had all the warmth of binary code. The relationship was primarily an electronic one. See, Wal-Mart's employees can scan any of the tens of thousands of product codes and get instant information on pricing, inventory, and sales history. Vendors are hooked into the same computer network. We could tap into Wal-Mart's inventory of ThighMasters any time we wanted to. In fact, Wal-Mart encouraged us to do so. The inventory was even broken down into how many weeks' supply the stores had based on sales from the prior day. It was amazing. It was also possible to tap into the scanners in the stores and watch how many units of any product were being sold.

This technology ensures fast turnover. Wal-Mart doesn't get stuck with product. The stores don't have large inventories because they're keeping such close tabs and they're getting deliveries from manufacturers *just in time*. That way, they force the manufacturers to hold onto the inventory for them.

At the other end of the spectrum was Woolworth. The company's loose inventory and distribution system could wreak havoc on the store managers, who ended up with a lot of product piled up in the back room or no product and empty shelves. Enter ThighMaster, a fast-seller, and they were pulling out their hair: The store managers ended up calling us directly to circumvent their own warehouse!

Looking back, I started in this business with no direct-response experience, no retail sales experience, and 18 months later, we staged one of the most successful new product launches of the decade, certainly one of the top launches from a small privately held company. We held sales records at Wal-Mart and Kmart, and at Target and Woolworth.

The point is, if you have any kind of retail sales operation you're way ahead of the game. Farther along than I was when I started. So don't let producing an infomercial scare you away from using direct response as a national media campaign for your product. The advantages are just too great. For example, even after the ad became unprofitable soon after we went retail in the fall of '91, I kept it on the air for another year just to drive my retail sales. The 20 percent who bought the ThighMaster on television almost completely financed the media campaign, which was all they were supposed to do. We made our profit just as I planned, from the 80 percent who bought the ThighMaster in retail stores.

Nor should you think this is a one-time phenomenon. Look at the broad retail success of infomercial products that came along after ThighMaster: Dura-Lube and the Abflex Exerciser. The Smart Mop and Perfect Smile Tooth-Whitener.

Of course, going retail changed everything. It meant jumping from six employees to forty in a couple of months. It meant dealing with Wal-Mart, not Mrs. Jones in Boise, Idaho. It meant sales quadrupled, but overhead costs increased.

There were other changes, too. When you're in the direct-response business, you come into the office in the morning, check the figures from your fulfillment house and your inbound tele-marketing, look at next week's media schedule, telephone the star with the latest figures, then go to lunch. That's about it. Once it's up and running, the campaign really runs itself. It's like there is no company, just an infomercial. It is truly a virtual corporation.

But the downside is you have to "buy" every sale because if you're not buying media, you're not selling product. There is no such thing as a free ride on momentum in direct response.

Not so with retail. In stores, just being on the shelf may be all that's needed to sell the product, even after the heavy advertizing blitz is over. And when the chains start to run their own ads about your product and you see the displays, it's great. I mean, it's a hoot to go into your local store and see your product piled to the ceiling.

I tended to go on weekends. I'd jump in the car and drive to the Target in Culver City, on Jefferson Boulevard, not far from the old MGM studios.

At the entrance, I'd run into a chest-high pyramid of ThighMas-ters. From there, I'd make a beeline to the back of the store to check the aisle displays. I'd look to see how many ThighMasters were left. I also checked out the competition, that is, other fitness products. I'd ask a clerk or two how things were going.

I'd linger a while and watch the customers pushing their red plastic shopping carts down the aisle. I always hoped to catch one in the act of choosing the ThighMaster. I was rarely disappointed.

She—the customer was nearly always a she—would reach for the ThighMaster, turn the box over in her hands, then drop it into the cart with the $10 iron, the floral throw pillows, pet supplies, Hanes briefs, Dodgers T-shirt, and the half dozen toddler tumblers.

All the months of hard work were worth this one, delicious moment.

Mission accomplished, I'd head out the door, but not before buying a bag of popcorn. One time, as I was getting into my car, juggling the keys, the popcorn, and some laundry detergent, two young women parked next to me were arguing. The debate centered on who owed whom $1.50. This, despite the fact that they were loading what looked like several hundred dollars' worth of merchandise into the trunk of a Mercedes.

In some twisted way, the scene reminded me of the story Dorothy Parker told about walking out of the Garden of Allah, a glorious old hotel on Sunset Boulevard, long since demolished. As Parker walked out into the sunshine, a long, black limousine pulled up. The window rolled down to reveal a graceful hand, sheathed in an evening glove, holding . . . a half-eaten bagel.

I love L.A.

CHAPTER · 8

●●●

A Cultural Icon

A lot of people made fun of the ThighMaster, and I'm glad that they did.

Jay Leno [introducing gift ideas]: "This is the ThighMaster Orange Juice Squeezer. [He picks up a ThighMaster and squeezes an orange with it.] Now you can have great-lookin' legs *and* fresh juice. . . ."

David Letterman: "Let me begin tonight's telecast with some good news. The United States Surgeon General has now indicated that using the ThighMaster is safe sex."

Diane White, a columnist for the *Boston Globe* [on uses for the ThighMaster, other than exercising, for people like her who bought one but never use it]: "As a jack, in an emergency, if you have a very small car. . . . As a rack to dry homemade pasta. . . . Prop it on its side and presto! Twin picture frames. . . . Have it bronzed and claim it's a very early Henry Moore. . . ."

Even President Bush got into the act with a joke about his overweight press secretary, Marlin Fitzwater, using our product.

The ThighMaster became a sensation with numerous personal appearances on television and in movies. Katie Couric, Joan Lunden, and Paula Zahn chipped in to give Candace Bergen a ThighMaster on *Murphy Brown,* to get in shape after the birth of her baby. Bernice held one up in *Designing Women* and knocked it, saying: "You know, I've been trying out this ThighMaster, and it's just not happening for me, although I am able to crack a nut between my knees." Rita Rudner and Emma Thompson work out with one in *Peter's Friends,* and one of Damon Wayans' misfit recruits tries to get in shape with one in *Major Payne.*

The infomercial made appearances, too. In *Forever Young,* Mel Gibson awakens to the ThighMaster ad on television after being frozen for 50 years. In *Made in America,* Whoopi Goldberg and Ted Danson are caught making out by her daughter while Suzanne works our product on the TV behind them.

But the most effective PR was Suzanne's appearances on the TV talk shows. She started with Steve Edward's former morning show in Los Angeles. She wasn't there to talk about ThighMaster, but she worked it into the conversation. Next thing I knew, I got a call from West Telemarketing. The phones were on fire. People had actually called the TV station to find out how they could get a ThighMaster and the station gave them our 800 number. I was amazed that many people went to so much trouble.

Then, she hit the big ones, *Donahue, The Maury Povich Show, Live with Regis and Kathie Lee,* and *Larry King Live,* among many others.

Suzanne [smiling] "See, you could be using the ThighMaster right now while you're sitting there interviewing me. It could just be there between your knees, back and forth, and your thighs would be rock-hard like mine" [Giggles].

Larry King [incredulous] "Wait a minute. Are you telling me that you are currently, at this second, using your ThighMaster?"

She made an appearance on *Late Night with David Letterman*—and I do mean appearance. Alan called me and said the Letterman show wanted Suzanne for the opening monologue. The idea was, she'd be backstage, sitting on a stool, exercising with the Thigh-Master, and Dave would hear her breathy counting. He'd walk back to investigate and—surprise!—find Suzanne Somers.

"You mean she's not a guest?" I asked.

"That's right," said Alan. "That's what makes it so funny."

So, we flew her to New York. Sure enough, the bit went over great.

Celebrities who are good at patter—and not all of them are—are welcome on morning talk shows and syndicated shows like *Oprah,* although usually to talk about their current series, new gossip, a worthwhile cause, and so forth. (Few shows booked Suzanne because they wanted her to promote the ThighMaster.) So the real challenge is successful *bridging.* This is a term media people use to cover the sly art of changing the subject when the interviewer is asking the wrong questions.

Many politicians "cross the bridge" multiple times in any interview, but with ham-fisted subtlety. There's about a football field's length of daylight between the question and the answer:

Mike Wallace: "Senator, how do you respond to reports that you were videotaped accepting a bribe at 9:32 P.M. on Nov. 14th?"

Senator: "Anybody can say anything they want, Mike. That's what I love about this country—the first amendment. But more important than the right of free speech is the purity of our water. Our children's health depends on it. Let me tell you about the bill I've introduced. . . ." and off he goes until Wallace, having heard enough, rolls the incriminating videotape.

Actors are more subtle. The ones who are media savvy deftly change the subject, from old TV shows to what they're selling; from tabloid headlines to what they're selling; from past successes to—that's right—what they're selling. And no one's better at that than Suzanne Somers.

What made the PR for the ThighMaster so effective was that Suzanne played it straight. With great warmth and enthusiasm she described what a wonderful product the ThighMaster was. Everyone around her would read the double entendres into what she was saying. It wouldn't have worked as well if she was some serious physical fitness guru. Double entendres with Kathy Smith or Cathy Rigby are nowhere near as much fun as double entendres with Suzanne Somers. Here was this gorgeous blonde, with this very sexy image, squeezing this thing between her legs, yet doing it with a straight face. Suzanne was perfectly happy to play dumb, to distance herself from the sexiness of the product. Everyone around her would be making wisecracks while Suzanne, smiling sweetly, would carry on about how many repetitions you need to do. It worked like gangbusters.

Suzanne is wonderfully telegenic, and although the general public may think she's on talk shows all the time, she turns down most requests to make appearances. So when she has something important to promote or to say, she is easy to book. She clusters her appearances on numerous shows over a short period of time. When she's on a PR tour, it seems she's on TV every time you turn it on. She did it with her books, with ThighMaster, and ButtMaster, the exercise product she introduced in the fall of 1995.

She is not working alone. Alan, her husband and manager, the former talk-show host, is also very media savvy. He did most of the work setting up her appearances for the ThighMaster, and he did an excellent job.

My only problem with Suzanne's performance was that she consistently exaggerated her role in the ThighMaster success story at the expense of Ovation. Finally, the company dropped out of her patter altogether, and she reported that Anne-Marie Bennstrom brought her the product directly, that she and Alan loved it, and the rest was history.

The ThighMaster clicked with the public but became more than a hot product. Fat-free cookies and over-the-counter heartburn pills are hot products, but comedians are not peppering their monologues with cookie jokes and no one around the water cooler is boasting about rushing out to buy Tagamet HB or Pepcid AC. In other words, these products are not playing on the most important network in America: the word-of-mouth network. Too bad no ad agency can guarantee a booking on it. Such an agency could buy Madison Avenue out of its hip pocket.

Fads are born of a combination of advertising and publicity, which is more than the sum of the two parts. Advertising spreads the word and asks for the order; PR humanizes the product and builds credibility. Money can buy you advertising, but it can't guarantee good PR. The product cameos and mentions in TV episodes and movies that vault your product into the fad hall of fame come unsolicited. Other kinds of publicity depend on a quick response to an unusual situation, like the time the California National Guard worked out with our product thanks to Jonathan Noel.

Noel was a friend of Josh's who had independently produced an exercise video for use with the ThighMaster. During the Los Angeles riots of 1992, when troops were called in to protect the city, soldiers were doing a lot of standing around while they waited for assignments to trouble spots. Their officers had them exercise to pass the time. Jonathan saw a need. He grabbed about fifty special edition ThighMasters, threw 'em into his car, and sped to the Crenshaw Shopping Center, which was one of the staging areas. Along the way, he picked up four aerobic instructors. Later that night there was film on Fox, KTLA and KABC of soldiers in fatigues jumping up and down with ThighMasters, and four women in leotards showing them the moves. The soldiers seemed to love it, and, needless to say, we loved the exposure.

Wherever I went, I saw the ThighMaster. Whenever I turned on the television or went to the movies, I saw the ThighMaster.

It was a heady experience.

I remember a black-tie fundraiser Randee and I attended in L.A. at the height of the ThighMaster craze. It was at the Beverly Wilshire Hotel, a wonderful old hotel at the end of Rodeo Drive where all kinds of splashy society events are held. I wore a tux, of course, and Randee wore a long, black evening gown. We arrived late and were seated at a table where a couple had failed to show. It turned out to be an "in" table, at least by Hollywood standards: The husbands were all entertainment attorneys. Because their clients included movie companies, stars, and recording artists, the conversation focused on advances, foreign-rights deals, merchandising deals, and so on. Why was Harrison Ford's lastest pulling better in Japan than the most recent Sly Stallone vehicle? And how about those new fast-food tie-ins in England? (The lawyers make out like bandits on action films, since each project has a mess of deals attached to it. There ain't much merchandising potential in *Henry V.*)

One of the wives looked bored, and I couldn't blame her. There are only so many ways you can slice a Stallone deal, and I suspect she knew about all of them. She turned toward me, a hopeful look on her face. What did I do? she wanted to know. I told her I sold things on television, which is what I usually said when someone asked me what I did for a living. (I never knew what to say, frankly. Infomercials are such an odd thing to be successful at.)

Her face brightened. But before she could utter another word, the attorney on Randee's left whipped around and said that one of his clients, an actress, had been approached to be a spokesperson for an infomercial. The bored wife pounced. "Well," she said. "Wouldn't it be nice if she hit the jackpot like Suzanne Somers!"

I mentioned casually that the ThighMaster was my company's product.

It was like Dean Witter had called. All conversation stopped dead in its tracks. Everyone turned toward me. *How did it happen? Tell us about Somers' deal. Did I invent the product? How much is Suzanne making? Is her deal normal in the infomercial business? How much is the inventor making?*

Now one of the attorneys announced that his wife had *actually purchased* something from television, a SnackMaster. The wife blushed and giggled and waved him away but he continued, with much gusto, about how he loved the product, how it grilled sandwiches in seconds, how convenient it was to have it in their master suite. (A lot of houses in Beverly Hills have master suites with his-and-her bathrooms. They're sometimes equipped with tiny refrigerators and microwaves in case the couple wants a late-night nosh. It's too far to traipse to the kitchen, of course, and you don't wake the maid at 2 A.M.)

The way the guy told the story, it was like his wife had done something truly exotic like go to a fortune teller or a nude beach.

For the rest of the evening, infomercials dominated the conversation. One woman thought her psychotherapist had charisma enough to project well on TV and that it was important his message about parenting yourself reach as many people as possible. *What did I think?* Between spoonfuls of mango sorbet, one of the attorneys told me about a golf gadget his pro had given him that he swore took four strokes off his score, and he was pretty sure he could get Arnie for an endorsement. *What did I think?*

What did I think? I thought the sorbet was divine.

Epilogue

Until ThighMaster, manufacturers rarely considered infomercials as a legitimate marketing tool. It's easy to see why. There's a whiff of carpetbag about the way infomercial marketers hop opportunistically from one product category to another, from lipsticks to screwdrivers to knitting machines. These people are loyal to the *process,* not the product. They're always looking for new grist for the mill.

Mainstream manufacturers are different. They're usually heavily invested in a single product category. They spend money on R & D. They have a loyal customer base. They go to their industry conventions; they belong to their industry trade groups. (By and large, infomercial people go to NIMA's convention.) To manufacturers, there's something unsavory about someone who's raised selling to a high art and for whom the product is secondary.

I thought the same thing until I realized an infomercial campaign could be used as a marketing strategy in the early life of a brand and that I didn't have to become Ron Popeil to do so.

ThighMaster showed how a tiny company lacking the resources for a national TV campaign could buy a big TV presence with direct-response advertising. Today, start-ups and established manufacturers are adopting this strategy: BreathAsure, Comfort Trac (the Contour Pillow folks), Merle Norman Cosmetics, and Health Rider, are among the many companies remaining in their product categories using direct-response as advertising.

These companies are opening the door, but others should enter. If you're a small manufacturer with a product with mass appeal, you should consider using infomercial marketing strategies to build brand equity. This is particularly true if your product has a competitive advantage that demonstrates well on TV.

As I scan the infomercial horizon, I see some other trends.

More use of infomercials by large, traditional television advertisers. The large, traditional television advertisers who want to go beyond the thirty-second soundbite are moving rapidly and aggressively into direct response. I'm talking about companies such as Apple Computers, Fidelity Investments, and Motorola. Microsoft introduced Windows 95 in an infomercial that starred *E.R.*'s Anthony Edwards.

Even car companies, slaves of conventional advertising, are using infomercials. Chrysler ran a long-form infomercial as a lead generator for its 1994 Dodge Ram pickup truck because the company needed the time to point out its luxurious features, unexpected in a pickup truck, and to demonstrate the truck's technical prowess. The infomercial's production values were on par with its expensive image spots, but the sales pitch had the depth of a multipage brochure. There was time to tout details like slide-away cup holders and storage space for a laptop computer and compare the torque of four different engines. At the end of the show, Chrysler ran an 800 number for people who wanted more information. The purpose of many lead-generation shows is to collect names and phone numbers of potential buyers to pass along to local dealers for follow-up.

In 1993, Mattel introduced Classique Barbie, a limited edition of specially commissioned Barbie dolls. The target audience was adults who collect dolls. (Don't laugh; there are 50,000 Barbie collectors alone.) The show was hosted by Pam Dawber, who interviewed the dolls' designers and a handful of Barbie collectors. Mattel felt it needed the thirty-minute format to get across the quality and detail that went into the dolls. (I know something about this because I was a consultant on the show.) They zeroed in on real zippers and rooted eyelashes and the luxurious fabrics used for the dolls' ballgowns.

It's a trend that is likely to continue. *Advertising Age,* in conjunction with NIMA, hired ASI Market Research to do a study of nationally branded products in infomercials. The study found that close to 13 percent of nationally branded advertisers surveyed, produced an infomercial in 1995 to sell products or services. During the next three years, that number is expected to jump to 30 percent. Of those advertisers surveyed, nontraditional media, of which infomercials are a part, accounted for only 3 percent of their budget. However, that number is expected to grow dramatically as the number of infomercials increases.

Oddly, many national manufacturers are not taking full advantage of the benefits of direct response. They designate a certain amount of money to the direct-response campaign just as they would to a traditional advertising campaign. Then, they pull the plug when they exhaust the budget. That makes sense in traditional advertising, where an ad budget represents an investment in future profits, but direct-response cash flow makes it a horse of a different color: The ad budget is financed out of the campaign's positive cash flow. Whether you're a small manufacturer or a Fortune 500 company, work it like traditional direct response. Keep the ad on the air as long as it's profitable.

More major hits from entrepreneurial infomercial producers. The infomercial industry is still ripe for start-up entrepreneurs with a direct-response career in mind. Year after year, despite rising media rates, greater regulation, and greater competition, start-up entrepreneurs are generously represented in the top shows. Alien Ultimate Wedge (a golf club), Smart Mop, Smart Chopper, Topsy Tail, Komputer Tutor, Miracle Thaw, the list goes on and on. Start-up costs in this industry remain modest, and the network of vendors who can help newcomers avoid mistakes is growing bigger and bigger.

Increasing polarization between the larger, more corporate TV marketers, like American Telecast and Guthy-Renker, and old-style TV spokespeople, like Mike Levey, Tony Hoffman, and Ron Popeil. Infomercial companies like Guthy-Renker and American Telecast will produce ever more expensive shows, backed up by thorough focus group and market research. (Look at the production values of *Mon Amie Cosmetics,* starring Kathie Lee Gifford, or the latest *Personal Power* show, starring Anthony Robbins.) Although these companies appear to have a lot in common with traditional TV pitch guys—they jump opportunistically from one product category to another; they enter a product category without intending to stay there beyond the life of their infomercial campaign; they devote insignificant funds to R & D and to going retail—they shy away from goofy products like Popeil's hair-in-a-can. Bigger isn't better, but it remains classier.

More infomercials promoting social causes. The religious right built a powerful base of contributors and activists with the help of short-form infomercials about Vietnam MIAs and abortion; their emotional ads on these highly charged issues raised support for the full range of their agenda. For a variety of reasons, liberals have failed to capitalize on TV's ability to rally the troops. Yet infomercials could be used effectively by such special interest groups as the gun control lobby, the antitobacco lobby, and the pro-choice lobbies.

Traditionally, advocacy groups have raised funds and sought new members with direct-mail pieces, which, of course, reach only one person or a household. The beauty of direct-response TV is that, when people phone in, not only can their names can be added to a petition that's going to Congress, but they can be asked to contribute money to keep the TV campaign on the air. Those who respond to the ad pay for a message that is seen by millions of other people who catch it while changing channels. This is how you bring others into the tent. This is how you can preach to the unconverted.

The battle for the hearts, minds, and pocketbooks of American voters is bound to heat up as more and more special interest groups take advantage of the power of television, and specifically infomercials.

Where am I now? I left Ovation in early 1993. Pippa and I disagreed about the direction of the company. We each tried to buy the company from the other. Negotiations deteriorated, and our relationship soured. Pippa held the upper hand and ended up buying my stock and settling my contract. I've had little further contact with the company.

I spent the next few months feeling distressed and angry. I thought I was building a company that would be around a very long time and I'd run it until the day I retired. It was not to be. Then, a year and half after I left, much to my surprise, the company went bankrupt. What happened? How could a healthy, vibrant and growing enterprise collapse so quickly? I don't know. I wish I did.

I don't spend a lot of time mulling it over now. I've certainly weathered career changes before and prospered afterwards.

Today, I have two new companies, both located in Hollywood. Bieler Marketing Associates is an advertising agency that helps both entrepreneurs and established companies build sales and brand equity using the cheap infomercial marketing strategies I've discussed in this book. Some clients come to us for direction through the entire process, from market research, through production, all the way to foreign distribution. Others want help with just a few steps—copy strategy, for instance, or bridging into retail, or signing a celebrity spokesperson.

I also have Media Funding Corporation, which funds media purchases for those who've had successful tests. Yes, you can finance a campaign out of cash flow, as I did with ThighMaster, but some people want to roll out more quickly using third-party money. MFC is for them. Clients maintain control of their campaigns and MFC's fees are blended into the media agency's fees, so they have minimal impact on a client's bottom line. The client is also relieved of the media risk because, with few exceptions, MFC relies on the campaign's performance to recoup its media advances.

Both companies are flourishing, and I enjoy helping others move ahead in the business. But sometimes in the middle of the night I lie awake and fantasize about doing it all over again—finding another product, and starting and building another Ovation. Setting out on a wild adventure. Again.

But I won't because it took such a toll the first time. I worked ridiculously long hours, and for three years, I was never not tired. I also rarely saw my family. My daughter complained about going to bed before I got home and waking up after I left in the morning.

But she did have the final say on the subject. It was at the signing ceremony that marked my departure from the company. There were a half dozen attorneys around a conference table and, after a long morning of last-minute negotiations, papers were signed and checks were transferred. About that time, Holly, then 2½, burst in and climbed onto a chair. Her red dress was the only splash of color in the room. Unintimidated by the tense, unsmiling faces, she announced in a clear, decisive voice when I laid down my pen, "I'm taking my Daddy home now."

She did, and she kept me there. I protect my weekends now so I can spend more time with Randee and the kids. That's right, kids. Randee and I had another baby. A girl. Her name is Lacey Rose.

Our house feels rather cramped these days. We still love it, and the neighborhood, too, but we know it's time to move out. And up. Closer to Nicolas Cage and farther from Brad Pitt. I only hope there's a house in the Hills that offers both a view of the city and of Holly's beloved sign.

Peter's TimeLine

Here is a checklist of steps you must take to put together a successful infomercial campaign. The process is covered fully in the book, but an abbreviated list can help you make sure nothing is overlooked.

I am also providing you with some leads to companies that can help you maximize your profits after a successful test. (If you want a current list, give us a call at Bieler Marketing Associates in Hollywood, and we will try to set you straight.)

The first challenge is to find the right product. If you already have your eye on something, evaluate it before you spend money developing a campaign. Check chapter three for my guidelines on product selection. Then, check out the competition. You may be surprised to find that someone else tried to sell a product similar to yours—and because the infomercial flopped, you never heard of it. And it is easy to do. Jordan Whitney Inc. tracks all the infomercials that play on national cable, including those elusive ones that play only a few times in test, never to be seen again. Check out their published reports, and plan to buy video copies of any shows you can learn from. They are located in Tustin, CA.

If you uncover a failed potential competitor, study their effort in depth. Get past the obvious blemishes. Most infomercials fall short creatively, but lots of shows with mediocre performances and unimaginative camerawork do gangbusters, so don't dismiss the failure as the result of lackluster production values, even if that is the case. The elements that really make a difference, like the offer and the creative strategy, are discussed in chapter two.

Stay away from products with complicated offers—a wide selection of sizes or colors, for instance. There are three good reasons for this: (1) Your inbound telemarketing costs will zoom while your clients dawdle on the phone trying to choose; (2) you could suffer disastrous returns from people who found the product did not exactly match their needs (like all the unhappy consumers who returned their hair extenders because the product did not exactly match their natural hair color); and (3) your inventory costs are multiplied many times, and this can be a problem for a start-up entrepreneur.

Remember the ratios. In the low price ranges (say under $50.00) you need a minimum of a 4-to-1 ratio between your cost of manufacturing or purchase and your consumer price. At higher price points, the ratio can loosen somewhat to 3 to 1. Without these spreads, you cannot reasonably expect to cover the costs of media, telemarketing, warehousing, and the like.

What is the best price point? One that produces an acceptable profit and has buyer appeal. Think of your product's value for the average person with a problem to solve. If you have a household cleaner you want to price at $19.95, does your product really solve a $20.00 problem? Do most people have a cheaper or easier way to solve the problem? If so, beware.

This is a new industry, but we have two active trade organizations that can be important sources of information, and you may want to join one of them while you are still in the planning stages. They both issue regular publications and hold conventions that provide comprehensive coverage on the industry for newcomers and veterans. NIMA (National Infomercial Marketing Association) is located in Washington, D.C. Direct Marketing Association is located in New York City.

Three publications track trends, personalities, and services in the business. Both *Response TV,* published in Santa Ana, CA, and *Steve Dworman's Infomercial Marketing Report* out of Los Angeles host important infomercial conventions. *Electronic Retailing,* a bimonthly glossy, is published by Creative Age Publications in Van Nuys, CA.

The second challenge is making the infomercial. There are many excellent production companies who will be happy to write, cast, and shoot your infomercial. But be careful, because their incentive is to get you into production as quickly as possible to generate fees. While the best ones will warn you of a poor product selection, for instance, or unrealistic pricing, you cannot count on them to address your marketing problems. I recommend starting with a direct-response advertising agency. (I head up one.) You are more likely to find experienced marketing people there. And because most of our fees are generated only after an infomercial is successful (media fees), we are more sensitive to problems we see going in.

And agencies can help you with production when it is time to roll cameras. We all keep tabs on the best freelancers and production houses to help you pick the right creative people for your product. And we are in a good position to comparison-shop production costs on your behalf. This useful separation of production companies from ad agencies has become blurred in the infomercial world, but it is the way Madison Avenue has been doing it for years. With good reason, I think.

I want to add a word of caution about stars. I have seen a few entrepreneurs lately caught up in a star's enthusiasm for the project which causes them to push ahead with troubled shows that ultimately fail. If you start having second thoughts, do not proceed just because you have interest from a celebrity. Celebrities learn a certain amount of marketspeak, but their experience is usually limited to marketing themselves. And very often, their enthusiasm for a project is based on factors that have very little to do with your success—for instance, how well the program will showcase them. It may be hard for a newcomer to dismiss a well-known star's opinion. But that's what needs to be done sometimes.

Then you must test the completed show. I recommend a two-stage test in chapter five. First you spend three to ten thousand dollars to get a feeling for the marketability of your product. (Some people break this investment into two stages, say an initial buy of three thousand followed by another seven a few weeks later.) If this initial test fails badly, you may want to write off the campaign. If the show is close to profitability but not the hit you want, you will probably vary the price point or payment plan and engage in some creative tweaking before testing again. As part of this second stage you may need to buy comparative A and B tests (same infomercial except for one element, say the price, running in two different but similar markets.)

One of the most frequent misconceptions I deal with at Bieler Marketing Associates is about the size of inventory you need to back up a test. The figure is usually in the hundreds, not the tens of thousands. If you are buying five thousand dollars worth of media to test a $49.95 product, and your allowable is $25.00, then you need about 250 units in the warehouse to satisfy the expected orders. ($5,000 divided by the $25.00 allowable plus an extra 500 units.) And don't buy or produce much more, unless you have a clear way of liquidating them if the show does not work.

Always engage a major telemarketer and credit-card processor to handle your account. They will be used to working together and exchanging information electronically. Your ad agency can help you get set up with them. They will also set you up with duplicators who specialize in copying infomercials and "bicycling" them to TV stations and cable networks.

Your media buyers, whether independent or part of an agency, will be responsible for two processes crucial to your success: (1) Buying time that hits your target market at the best rates; and (2) reporting back to you on the success of each of these broadcasts, so you can adjust your buys to stay profitable. Profitability is calculated by taking the orders generated by each broadcast (stations broadcast different phone numbers to make the task easier) and relating this amount back to the cost of the media buy. When you are choosing media buyers, make sure they show you the reports they will be sending you. Are they clear? How soon after a broadcast will they be issued? (See chapter five for more details.)

Hooray! You have a successful test. You have overcome the biggest challenge of all. Creating a successful campaign. But now it is time to roll out, and you have a new set of problems. First of all, your media buyers will be calling you to write them checks. Big checks. Maybe as much as $350,000 a week. You can tell them to expand slowly so you can finance your "ramp-up" out of cash flow. But if you want to expand quickly, you will need to make a further investment. If you want to use outside money, you can turn to Media Funding Corporation, my company in Hollywood, whose business it is to help companies in exactly this situation.

Your next challenge is to get set for retail. As you know, Ovation hired its own sales force, but there are a number of good companies who will be more than happy to do it for you. Telebrands in Fairfield, NJ handles retail for a lot of infomercial companies. (Yup, my old adversary A. J. Khubanni.) Fitness Quest in Canton, OH is entering the field. Mike Clark, who did such a good job for us at Ovation, now works there. Direct to Retail in Framingham, MA has also enjoyed a lot of success introducing infomercial hits into stores.

While retail is the biggest market for most successful infomercial products, there are several other markets you should not overlook. Here are a few.

Print direct. National Syndications Inc. in New York City can run ads for your product in Sunday supplements like Parade or USA Weekend. They can also run an FSI campaign. (FSI is short for Free Standing Inserts, which are the glossy coupons which fall out of your Sunday paper—a bigger business than a cursory glance would suggest.) They will sometimes run ads at their own expense, and buy product from you.

Credit card syndicators. These companies advertise your product on inserts in credit-card statements (bank, oil, department store, and the like). They will often foot the costs of the inserts and buy product from you for a discount off wholesale. Talk to Media Syndication Global in New York, and Santa Barbara Promotions in Santa Barbara, CA.

The shopping channels. These are important accounts, but their importance is sometimes overrated by newcomers to the field. HSN and QVC combined post gross annual sales of about $2.5 billion. Wal-Mart alone does over $50 billion. Sell to them, obviously, but do not make them the focus of your marketing effort.

Catalogues. According to the Direct Marketing Association, catalog sales to consumers climbed to $38.6 billion in 1995, and the mass-market mailers like Harriet Carter or Walter Drake are hungry for hot TV products. Contact them directly, or work through a broker like Catalog Solutions in Westport, CT.

That's it. That's all I've got to say. The Fedex guy is standing by to take this to our publisher.

Good luck. Godspeed. And stay in touch.

Index

Miami Beach, 62
Micro Crisp, 30
Microsoft, 180
middle class, 52–53
Milchan, Arnon, 42
Miller Lite, 17
Millionaire Maker, 30
Mindpower, 43
Miracle Blade, 73
Miracle Thaw, 182
Mirchandani, Keith, 138
Mishan, Eddie, 136, 137–138,
    139, 146
Mon Amie Cosmetics, 182
Money-Making Secrets, 74
Monroe, Marilyn, 86, 109,
    119–120
Morris, Arnold, 64
Motorola, 180
movie producing, 19–20
Murphy Brown, 170
Muscle & Fitness, 25
Muscle Beach, 39
Myers, Jim, 129, 140–149

Nashville Network, 43
National Infomercial Market-
    ing Association (NIMA),
    13, 28, 52, 129, 179, 181,
    189
National Media, 53
National Syndications Inc., 191
NBC, 40, 110
negative response campaign,
    116
Nelson, Craig T., 89

net deals, 93
New Generation, 29
New Haven, 114
New York Times, 41
Newark, 141–142
Nichols, Mike, 19
NIMA. *See* National Infomer-
    cial Marketing Associa-
    tion
Nimoy, Leonard, 12, 21
900 numbers, 74, 118
Nissan, 30
Nostalgia, 43
Notaro, Tony, 63–64, 67–68,
    70–72

O'Brien, Hugh, 23
O'Connor, Sinead, 12
Odyssey, 24
Ogilvy, David, 4
Omaha, 111, 114, 122
Oprah, 171
Orange County Swap Meet,
    155–156
Oshman's, 158
outsourcing, 46–47, 51,
    110–112
Ovation, 52, 102, 119, 122, 123,
    134, 143, 144, 172, 183,
    184, 191
Owens, Gary, 21

Palm Springs, 91
Pan, Hermes, 40
Parker, Dorothy, 166
Parks, Jack, 31–32, 39, 47

Volvo, 17
V-Partners, 144
V-Toner, 76–77, 80–81, 86, 87,
    95
Vu, Tom, 23

Wagner, Robert, 73
Wal-Mart, 4, 47, 139, 158–159,
    161–166, 192
Walter Drake, 192
Walton, Sam, 162
The Waltons, 41
The War of the Roses, 42
Warwick, Dionne, 89, 90
Wayans, Daman, 170
Wayne, John, 40
Wednesday's Children, 88
Weider, Joe, 26, 39
Welch, Raquel, 74
West Palm Beach, 114

West Telemarketing, 114–115
White, Diane, 169
White, Vanna, 74
Wiest, Dianne, 41
Williams, Katie, 30
Williams Television Time, 30
Windows 95, 5, 180
Winfrey, Oprah, 79
Witter, Dean, 174
Wood, Ed, 74
Wood, Natalie, 40, 120
Woolworth, 158, 159, 161, 164
word-of-mouth, 172–173

Yates, Peter, 107

Zahn, Paula, 170
Zanuck, Darryl F., 120
Zeffirelli, Franco, 107
Zimbalist, Efram Jr., 23

John Wiley & Sons, Inc. & Success Magazine Contest Application

Does your business have legs?

Enter this contest and find out.

If you've got a product to sell on TV, marketing genius and author Peter Bieler wants to hear about it.

Grand Prize

Enter the "this business has legs" contest and you may qualify for the Grand Prize, an expense-paid, 3-day/2-night trip for two to the legenday La Costa Resort and Spa in southern California and a weekend consultation with infomercial and marketing expert Peter Bieler (see reverse side for contest details).

How to Enter

Fill out the official order form and submit a description of your product, explaining how it is used and its consumer benefits. Please keep your description to 500 words or less.

Name _____

Address _____

Occupation _____

City, State _____

Phone Number _____

Tell us how you heard about this book and/or the contest.
( ) advertisement
( ) bookstore (name of bookstore)
( ) *Success* magazine

Please attach your proposal (500 words or less) and send to the following address by August 30, 1996:

Send to:
John Wiley & Sons, Inc.
P.O. Box 4313
Manhasset, NY 11030

1. You may enter by mailing the completed official entry form or providing the same information on a plain piece of paper, or you can access www.wiley.com/bieler.html. on the World Wide Web. Each contestant must write a description of a product, including how it is to be used and its consumer benefits, in not more than 500 words. Attach your name and complete address to your proposal. Mail your entry to: John Wiley & Sons, Inc. P.O. Box 4313, Manhasset, NY 11030. All entries must be received by August 30, 1996. John Wiley & Sons, Inc. is not responsible for late, lost, or misdirected postage. Your entry must be an original, unpublished creation and may not have won any award or be subject to any rights of any other parties. Sponsor reserves the right to verify the authenticity of each entry. All entries become the property of John Wiley & Sons, Inc. and will not be acknowledged or returned.

2. Entries will be judged by Peter Bieler, an infomercial expert, based upon the following criteria: Product Description 80% and Quality of Submission 20%. By entering this contest, each contestant agrees to be bound by these rules and the decision of the judge, which is final and binding.

3. Grand Prize: An expense-paid, 3-day/2-night trip for two to southern California at the legendary La Costa Resort and Spa. Trip includes round-trip air transportation from the major airport nearest the winner's home, hotel accommodations and a meal allowance (exlcuding alcohol) plus a consultation with Peter Bieler on an infomercial campaign, including test market design, marketing strategy, copy strategy, production and fulfillment planning. Trip subject to the schedule of Peter Bieler. No transfer or substitution for prize offered. Approximate Retail Value $5,000.00.

4. Winner will be notified by mail and must sign an affidavit of eligibility and release that must be completed and returned within 14 days or an alternate winner will be selected. Winner agrees to the use of the entry for advertising and publicity purposes without additional compensation, except where prohibited. Winner agrees that the sponsor, its affiliates, their agencies and employees, and Marden-Kane, Inc. shall not be held liable for any injury, loss, or damage of any kind resulting from participation in this contest or from acceptance or use of the prize.

5. Contest open to residents of the United States 18 years of age or older except employees and the immediate families of John Wiley & Sons, its subsidiaries, affiliates, agencies and Marden-Kane, Inc. All federal, state and local laws apply. Taxes, if any, are the responsibility of the prize winner.

6. For the name of the grand prize winner, available after November 30, 1996, send a self-addressed stamped envelope to: Laurie Frank, c/o John Wiley & Sons, 605 Third Avenue, New York, NY 10158.